T0089070

CHANGING PATTERNS OF
DELINQUENCY AND CRIME

CHANGING PATTERNS OF
DELINQUENCY AND CRIME

A Longitudinal Study in Racine

Lyle W. Shannon

with the assistance of:

**Judith L. McKim
Kathleen R. Anderson
William E. Murph**

Routledge
Taylor & Francis Group

LONDON AND NEW YORK

First published 1991 by Westview Press, Inc.

Published 2018 by Routledge
52 Vanderbilt Avenue, New York, NY 10017
2 Park Square, Milton Park, Abingdon, Oxon OX14 4RN

Routledge is an imprint of the Taylor & Francis Group, an informa business

Copyright © 1991 Taylor & Francis

All rights reserved. No part of this book may be reprinted or reproduced or utilised in any form or by any electronic, mechanical, or other means, now known or hereafter invented, including photocopying and recording, or in any information storage or retrieval system, without permission in writing from the publishers.

Notice:
Product or corporate names may be trademarks or registered trademarks, and are used only for identification and explanation without intent to infringe.

Library of Congress Cataloging-in-Publication Data
Shannon, Lyle W.
  Changing patterns of delinquency and crime : a longitudinal study in Racine / by Lyle W. Shannon.
    p. cm.
  Includes bibliographical references.
  ISBN 0-8133-8288-2
  1. Crime—Wisconsin—Racine—Longitudinal studies. 2. Juvenile delinquency—Wisconsin—Racine—Longitudinal studies. I. Title.
HV6795.R33S5 1991
364.3'6'0977596—dc20   90-25337
                                                                   CIP

ISBN 13: 978-0-367-01638-8 (hbk)

ISBN 13: 978-0-367-16625-0 (pbk)

Contents

Acknowledgments

So many people in Wisconsin and Iowa have worked so long on our various research projects on juvenile delinquency and crime that it is difficult to select those whose efforts applied to a specific research report, book chapter, journal article, or monograph. Involvement in the research on delinquency and crime commenced for some as early as 1972 and for others as recently as 1988. The names of those who played various roles in direction, analysis, data collection, coding, data manipulation, and report writing for four of the projects, "The Relationship of Juvenile Delinquency and Adult Crime to the Changing Ecological Structure of the City," National Institute of Justice Grant 79-JN-AX-0081, "A Processual Analysis of the Development of Continuities in Delinquency and Crime in High Delinquency and Crime Neighborhoods," National Institute of Juvenile Justice and Delinquency Prevention Grant 82-JN-AX-0004, "A More Precise Evaluation of the Effects of Sanctions," National Institute of Justice Grant 84-IJ-CX-0013, and "Prediction and Typology Development," National Institute of Justice Grant 85-IJ-CX-0019, are included in this brief acknowledgment.

Judith L. McKim has been involved in the earlier Racine research on the economic absorption and cultural integration of inmigrant workers since 1970 and then in the birth cohort research since 1972. She worked on the research design, instruments for data collection, data collection in Racine, and data processing, analysis, and report writing from the beginning. Supervision and training of the staff in both Iowa City and Racine has been her full time responsibility since 1970. She has assisted the principal researcher in writing and rewriting, cutting again and again, what some have considered to be all too lengthy reports to government agencies. This has always been difficult because almost every page seemed to be important in accounting for how we have arrived at the conclusions, some of which are so provocative.

Kathleen R. Anderson joined us in 1977 and has become more and more involved in the analysis and report writing. Her chapters from several research reports made a major contribution to understanding the complexity of the connection between juvenile delinquency and adult crime and the problem of errors in prediction.

Emily J. Meeks (deceased), James Curry, William F. Skinner, Lawrence Haffner, and William E. Murph, although no longer at the Iowa Urban Community Research Center, carried out the computer analyses over many years of research, including those described in this monograph. Haffner's mapping and graphics expertise has added notably to our presentations. Murph's work on computer-generated typologies and delinquent and criminal careers plus his willingness to assist us in difficult computer analyses long after employment with Preventive Medicine at the University of Iowa Hospitals has been especially appreciated.

Rachel E. Pezanoski has been Field Director in Racine during every interviewing phase of our research and for much of the time that data were being collected in the Police Department and courts. Among others who were field supervisors at one stage or another of the research were Michael R. Olson, Barney K. Pauze, Victoria F. Davison, Delores Luedtke, and Susan Shemanske. The following were either graduate or undergraduate students involved in various coding and analytic activities: Barbara A. Carson, Hugh S. Espey, Cheryl L. Garland, Tina Yuk-Bing Abels, Shari Hessong Morgan, Shirley Nelson-Kilger, Tie-Hua Ng, Vijayan K. Pillai, Joanne Ament, Jane Perkins, Ruth Moderson, and Margaret L. Bruns. These students, mostly graduate at the time, came from numerous sociology, geography, history, and business administration departments. The list would be even longer were we to include those who obtained interviewing and coding experience during earlier stages of the research, students from the University of Iowa and from the University of Wisconsin-Parkside.

Of the many who assisted in secretarial, clerical, and tabular work are Julie Burton, Debi S. Schreiner, Regina Oni, Mary Kathleen Stockman Zimmerman, and Debra J. Cobb. The manuscript was produced in camera-ready form by Tammie Woellert of the University of Iowa's Weeg Computing Center.

Our research has spanned the period in which Leroy Jenkins was Chief of Police and has continued through the administrations of numerous others, among them James J. Carvino, George Christensen, and Karl A. Hansen, the current police chief. Sergeant Alan D. Baker, Records Division, has been particularly helpful to us in recent years.

Members of the Advisory Boards for the projects described were: Professors Roland J. Chilton (University of Massachusetts), Harwin L. Voss (University of Kentucky), Aubrey Wendling (San Diego State University), Marvin Wolfgang (University of Pennsylvania), Robert M.

Figlio (University of Pennsylvania), Terence P. Thornberry (State University of New York-Albany), and Don C. Gibbons (Portland State University). Their suggestions and guidance were always appreciated. It is unfortunate that we have never had adequate funds to follow up on all of the suggestions made by our distinguished colleagues. Professor Robert Nash Parker (University of Iowa) has advised us on some of the more complex analyses. Professors Toby Parcel and David A. Parton supported our analyses in times of need.

Iowa's Vice President for Research, Dr. Duane C. Spriestersbach, and Deans Dewey B. Stuit and Howard Laster of the College of Liberal Arts assisted in financial support of the projects, as did the National Institute of Justice and the National Institute of Juvenile Justice and Delinquency Prevention. Their financial support does in no way indicate their agreement or disagreement with the conclusions which are presented in this volume.

Lyle W. Shannon

Chapter 1

AN INTRODUCTION TO THE RESEARCH ON DELINQUENCY AND CRIME

History of the Racine Research

This book is the product of 35 years of research on delinquency and crime in Madison and Racine, Wisconsin. The project was first conceived in 1955 by Professor Thomas C. McCormick, statistician/demographer in the Department of Sociology and Anthropology at the University of Wisconsin. As the most research-oriented member of the department, he captured the attention of Michael Hakeem and the author and we eagerly accepted his invitation to participate in a study of the changing ecology of delinquency in Madison.

Although Professor McCormick was struck down by a heart attack soon after data collection had commenced in 1956, Hakeem and Shannon continued the Madison research. What encouraged us at the outset was the unflagging cooperation of then Chief of Police of Madison, the late Bruce Weatherly. Several years later in the 1950s the author became acquainted with Chief LeRoy C. Jenkins of the Racine Police Department, a chief who had established a records system which was comparable to that in Madison. At his suggestion, we established a similar research project in Racine. No one could have been more cooperative or more tolerant. At times we had more researchers in the Records Division twenty-four hours a day than did the police department. At least six chiefs of police in Racine have continued to support our work during all these years, including the present chief, Karl Hansen. Judge John C. Ahlgrimm of the Juvenile Court was the first member of the judiciary to not only support the research but read our reports and acknowledge their importance for those who must make decisions about the futures of youthful and adult offenders.

Professors Harwin L. Voss (University of Kentucky), Austin T. Turk (University of California, Riverside), Robert M. Terry (University of Akron), and Charles H. McCaghy (Bowling Green State University) were among many graduate students who became involved in what was to become the continuing Wisconsin studies of delinquency and crime, first in Madison and then in Racine. Each not only used the Madison and/or Racine data for their theses or dissertations but have gone far beyond what we were doing at that time, distinguishing themselves in the field of criminology.

The Orientation of This Volume

Writing about all of these years of research is, in some ways, the most exciting part of the experience. It is almost as if the concluding chapter draws the characters into a penthouse high above the city's busy harbor for an answer to the causes of crime. By putting all of the strings of evidence together, by bringing our research findings up to the present, we are beginning to understand how various types and patterns of delinquency, crime, and drug use or drug offenses are the product of human interaction in every-day life. There are still, however, unanswered questions which should and could be settled by continuing the research in Racine.

In some walks of life (sociologists call them societal groups) daily activities are organized around work; one's life beyond family and friends, and even among friends, consists of a pattern of behavior acquired in what for some is an exciting world of work. In many other groups life is not organized around work because either there is none or the work available is distasteful, demeaning, and almost surely indicative of little but a dreary life ahead. Obtaining a job, never a position, does not provide much of a thrill, even though it may supply sustenance and shelter. Retirement, freedom from work at some distant time, is all that can be dreamed of.

With a perspective that enables us to go beyond simplistic explanations which attempt to account for delinquency and crime by characterizing people as sick or, even simpler, by saying that they are criminal types, we can see how delinquency may be as normal as Scouting, some kinds of crime may be as normal as accounting or sales work, and drugs and liquor may be as much an organizing principle for one's life as gourmet cooking is to people who have been integrated into the larger society. This perspective is not new (nothing is completely new) but the research that we have been conducting has reinforced our view that continuing within a sociological framework will produce answers to today's behavioral mysteries--what we sometimes see as the fascinating but dark and incomprehensible side of human behavior.

As the story unfolds, we shall learn how we (all of us in the larger society) have played a part, although we do not engage in most of these miscreant activities, in creating the arenas in which they are generated and perpetuated. If we wish to be severe with ourselves, we must reflect on the fact that we have sometimes in our uninformed concern also been unwitting accomplices.

On a recent visit to five major cities in Brazil, the author was impressed with the fantastic differences in the level of living between millions of favela residents (hillside and bayside) and those who live high on different hills or in the lush valleys in homes of such shocking beauty as to seem almost unreal to an Iowan. He could not help but note the difference in housing near the beaches of Rio de Janiero, Copacabana, Ipanema, Leblon, and the housing to be found only a few blocks away, like the Gold Coast and the slums in Chicago, much of the latter still remaining even with recent years of gentrification. At the same time, the fear of crime was ever-present among not only Rio's residents but those in every other major metropolitan area. This was a problem which its residents saw as explainable not in structural terms but in terms of "these people." That is not to say, however, that the Brazilian experience is unique. What we saw there is similar to what may be seen in every other urban, industrial/commercial metropolis in the Americas, it is only that the fear of ordinary crime, street crime, has been so intensified in Brazil's shimmering, even awesome, urban metropolises.

While this may seem a divergence from the story of our research, it helps place what we shall describe in a sociological perspective which will permit better understanding of why so much attention has been paid to the structure and growth of the city, to its transition from small town to urban industrial, from homogeneity to heterogeneity, from lakeside serenity to urban conflict. Some of Racine's residents have not always seen our accounts of what goes on in the community as helpful in solving community problems. They are probably correct but accounts and descriptions of the complexity of relationships lead to understanding the nature of problems. Understanding must precede effective approaches to amelioration.

Although our research on delinquency commenced in Madison in 1956 and in Racine in 1960, it was not until 1974 that our longitudinal birth cohort studies were underway in Racine. The design of the research, definitions of variables, and analytic techniques will be described as the volume progresses. Suffice it to say at this point that there were a total of 6,127 persons in the three birth cohorts (1942, 1949, and 1955) and, of these, 4,079 had continuous residence in Racine, these constituting the group who were analyzed most intensely. Lengthy interviews were also conducted with samples totalling 889 persons from the 1942 and 1949 Cohorts.

Since 1974 the National Institute of Juvenile Justice and Delinquency Prevention and the National Institute of Justice have supported research proposals from the Iowa Urban Community Research Center. The first was about the relationship of juvenile delinquency to adult crime. A second project investigated the relationship of delinquency and crime to the changing ecological structure of the city. This was followed by research on the development of serious criminal careers and the delinquent neighborhood. The next project involved an evaluation of the effect of sanctions. Our fifth project dealt with prediction and typology development. Most recently we have been analyzing patterns of drug use and their relationship to delinquency and crime.

The Chapters Which Account for the Development and Persistence of Delinquency and Crime

The second chapter presents the theoretical and empirical foundations of the early Racine research. It commenced with the ideas which guided our first project and explains how the findings were not only related to them but how, as the project progressed, some support was found for a variety of sociological explanations.

Theories are sufficiently overlapping that propositions derived from them produce research findings that may be strongly supportive of two somewhat similar but supposedly competing theories. The trick is to set up the analysis so that all but one of the sets of competing propositions is rejected by the analysis. This sounds quite scientific but is not that easy if the tests of propositions derived from theories involve theories that were non-existent before the data were collected. Even more likely, a many-faceted and broadly structured research project may lend weak support to a number of major sociological theories while rejecting none; each relevant theory appears to account for some delinquency and crime.

The answer to accounting for delinquency and crime lies in developing an integrated theory which, as we shall come to see, commences with the ecology of the city and cultural deviance, proceeds through the social structure and social processes types of explanations, and then adds social psychological variables which account for differences that occur within groups of people in the larger structural framework. This involves the testing of hypotheses or propositions that have evolved from different levels of perception. Although the demographic variables, race/ethnicity and sex, are not explanatory in themselves, they do enable us to better understand how people are positioned in the larger structure of society and thus have quite different chains of experiences during the process of socialization, even throughout their lives.

Having presented our theoretical position which builds upon the empirical research of generations of sociologists who came before us, most notably from the University of Chicago, the incidence and prevalence of delinquency and crime are described within an ecological framework which demonstrates how the changing structure of the city produces changing patterns of delinquency and crime. Although much of these data have appeared in earlier articles and/or in *Criminal Career Continuity: Its Social Context* (Shannon, 1988), they are again presented in summary form to emphasize the importance of ecology as a starting point.

What is going on in the minds of juveniles and adults and their ensuing behavior brings them to the attention of the police. That this is mediated by what is going on in the minds of police officers and other justice system persons and plays a part in the chain of events in persons' lives is again emphasized in order that the reader understand what we mean by social processes and chains of experiences. How all of this was internalized by members of the 1942 and 1949 Cohorts is only briefly mentioned at the outset but is dealt with in more detail in a later chapter.

Data from the first project in Racine were supportive of, or at least consistent with, what would be expected based on various social structure theories, cultural deviance as represented by the ecological approach, and various subcultural theories. At the same time, the findings were consistent with what one would expect to find based on social process theories. One could go a step further by saying that social conflict theories are not inconsistent with some of the findings. Our interpretation of the findings and methodological problems that gave us concern explain why our theoretical and methodological focus developed as it did for the second project, which in turn led to the third project, and so on.

Chapter 3 continues the ecological analyses with comparison of the findings utilizing census tracts, police grid areas, natural areas, and neighborhoods as spatial units, concluding that the smaller and more homogeneous neighborhoods enable us to better capture the relationship of urban social structure to delinquency and crime and ensuing temporal changes. This is followed by analyses which indicate how cohort, age, and time period variation are related to major areas in the city, particularly as the inner city and interstitial neighborhoods are differentiated from other types of neighborhoods in terms of the incidence of offenses, offense seriousness, the incidence of police referrals, and severity of court sanctions. All of this leads to how the cyclical nature of events has culminated in some deviations from the basic pattern of delinquency and crime rates in urban/industrial cities even though the most striking and readily recognizable consequence has been the hardening of the inner city.

Using the Neighborhood Data to
Focus Attention on the Present

The neighborhood data are analyzed in even more detail in Chapter 4 where each of sixty-five neighborhoods is classified as more or less delinquency and crime producing. Persons residing in neighborhoods variously characterized in such a way (milieu effects) are shown to have had proportionately different justice system involvement. This leads us further and further toward delinquency and crime as the product of learning experiences rather than as inner compulsions of types of people who are distributed more or less evenly throughout the population. The detailed data presented in the various tables in this chapter reveal considerable consistency in ecological patterns from measure to measure and considerable continuity in delinquent and criminal careers, particularly in inner city and interstitial neighborhoods. Increasing severity of sanctions from cohort to cohort had its greatest impact on serious, Non-White offenders who resided in the inner city.

To this point the chapters have, in a sense, been rather simple because they have dealt with delinquency and crime per se, ignoring the fact that the process may differ between inner city, interstitial, and other types of neighborhoods, by sex, and by race/ethnicity. In Chapter 5 these complexities are explored utilizing both official and self-report data, concluding that even the effects of the process of intervention differ by race/ethnicity, sex, and inner city vs. other neighborhood of residence. Still the experience variables account for large proportions of adult offender seriousness among inner city males, White or Non-White (the two groups which would encapsulate most of Racine's structural underclass as it is now referred to).

The Effectiveness of the Justice System

The consequences of sanctions are examined in some detail in Chapter 6, the data again revealing that sanctions failed to result in specific deterrence and produced even more serious misbehavior in the following period, the more severe were the sanctions. No matter how the data are manipulated, we find little to please those who believe that early and severe sanctioning, particularly institutionalization, as a policy will deter juveniles from further delinquent behavior. Since this is an issue which has been controversial for many years, particularly for those on the firing line, considerable effort was made to produce a finding that would be of use to those who are involved in day-to-day decision-making. Aside from the conclusion that sanctions in themselves are ineffective, the data did suggest that frequency of intervention was related to less serious offender careers as time progressed. On the other hand, more success was attained in accounting for career continuity.

Type of Offender Careers and the Prediction Problem

Prediction and offender typology development has been one of our most challenging concerns. At the same time, it is one of the most frustrating problems for those who must categorize offenders in a meaningful way and from that predict their future behavior. Creating a typology of institutionalized offenders is not the same as creating a typology from an entire cohort. Institutionalized offenders are skewed toward the more serious types while most members of a cohort are found in the least serious types. Although a number of approaches to typology development are presented, their greatest usefulness is in delineating the most serious types of offenses (felons and Part I offenders). This, however, is done after the fact and a typology based on only the juvenile proportion of careers fails to predict the nature of adult careers without considerable error, as shown in Chapters 7 and 8.

The first eight chapters provide a background for the chapter which may be of the most current interest, Chapter 9, "Drug Offender Types and Their Relationship to the Ecology of the City." Here we investigate the relationship of juvenile drug use and juvenile drug offenses to delinquency and adult crime. Our emphasis is on the role of drugs and alcohol in other delinquent and criminal activities, since they are linked among a large proportion of the young people in the study as well as among adults. How the connection between drugs and alcohol, delinquency and crime, and continuity in delinquency and crime differs by types of residential areas is the major concern of this next-to-concluding chapter. It even further points to the importance of focusing our attention on the structure of society and on-going social processes if we are to understand how people come to behave and misbehave as they do.

Chapter 10 summarizes the findings and indicates why it is so difficult to control delinquency and crime. If it seems to be a bit of a let-down, this is because we are so hesitant to make the kinds of claims that many others find so easy. What we should do if we are seriously concerned about delinquency and crime may be costly but, as we suggest in the concluding chapter, no one who knows anything about delinquency and crime has said that there are simple solutions to such complex problems.

Chapter 2

ASSESSING THE RELATIONSHIP OF
ADULT CRIMINAL CAREERS TO JUVENILE CAREERS

The Theoretical and Empirical Background

The social and physical conditions of persons who resided in inner city slums and the demographic characteristics of persons who resided in them were once considered explanatory of delinquency, crime, and a multitude of other deviant behaviors that seemed to have their genesis in these neighborhoods. Moving beyond this strictly social structural position (the theory that the subculture and life conditions present in the slums and transitional neighborhoods generate delinquent and criminal behavior), various social process theories (differential association, drift, control, bonding, and labeling) led to hypotheses about how patterns of social interaction were also productive of deviant behavior, delinquency and crime in particular. Although these social processes worked to produce higher delinquency and crime rates in the inner city and transitional areas, they also operated in other types of areas but with less deleterious consequences.

From the viewpoint of those who accepted either social structure or social process explanations of delinquency and crime, demolishing the slums and constructing new housing, however desirable and laudable a goal, probably did little to solve the persistent social problems of areas whose residents had still not been integrated into the larger society. Although there was a period in the 1930s and 1940s when slum clearance was widely accepted as the equivalent of the new Jerusalem in urban areas, re-housing did little in itself to change the life chances or behavior of most inner city dwellers, nor did later approaches based on psychological or medical models of human behavior, approaches which concentrated on changing individuals through a variety of therapies.

High rates of delinquency and crime and continuity from delinquency to crime continued to be a characteristic of those who resided in the inner city even after turn-of-the-century housing was replaced by new high-rise apartments or other shoe box architecture. The inner city also remained the setting for delinquency and crime and a multitude of other deviant behaviors by persons other than its residents.

Following their descriptions of the social ecology of the city, the Chicago structural sociologists (Park, Burgess, and McKenzie, 1925; Burgess, 1925; McKenzie, 1933) first emphasized affinity with delinquency and crime as an explanation for its continuity. Affinity mean growing up in an area, usually inner city neighborhoods, where delinquency and crime were commonplace and where one's peers engaged in delinquent behavior and one's adult role models were involved in all manner of criminal behavior. The numerous publications by Shaw (1929, 1930, 1938), Shaw and Moore (1931), Shaw and McKay (1942), Thrasher (1936), and others extending into the 1960s (Chilton, 1964) set the stage for a generation of research in which affinity and then affiliation (group membership) were, in a sense, the dominant social structure and social process explanatory themes (Matza, 1969). Structure and process were the products of industrialization and urbanization.

While Shaw and McKay and others in the Chicago group concentrated on determining the facts, as Empey (1982) has pointed out in his textbook presentation of competing theoretical positions, the spatial distribution of delinquency and crime which they found could be interpreted within the subcultural/cultural deviance (social structure) framework or within the social disorganization/breakdown of social controls (social process) framework.

Whichever theory was supported by the Chicago data, the 1920s and 1930s were a period in which the development of delinquency and crime was explained within a sociological framework (Stark, 1987). The structure or organization of the community determined the kind of neighborhood in which one would be socialized in socioeconomic and in racial and ethnic terms, and to a considerable extent determined the life chances, educational, and occupational opportunities that one would have. While America had been a land of opportunity, there were also limitations, at least for a large proportion of those who were and who would remain at the lowest socioeconomic levels.

Our initial concern in Madison, Wisconsin was to determine if there was spatial variation in the distribution of delinquency rates in that community. Voss (1956) did find delinquency rates to be related to the social areas of Madison and was followed by McCaghy (1962) who showed how delinquency was similarly related to the ecology of Racine in much the same pattern as Shaw and McKay had earlier found in Chicago in the 1920s.

A variety of social structure explanations of delinquency and crime have been developed during the past fifty years and many have endured with modification. Social structure explanations did not then nor do they now entirely account for why some juveniles and some adults do or do not become delinquents and criminals but this level of explanation was and remains a good, perhaps the best, starting point. Although the distribution of official rates of delinquency and crime were closely related to the spatial distribution of the subculture to which people were exposed within their immediate nearby groups, understanding the importance of social structure was necessary but not sufficient for a complete accounting of how some people engage in delinquent and criminal behavior and others do not.

The next category of explanations, as we have indicated, dealt with social processes. Coterminous with the social structure work of that period, Sutherland (1939) went beyond affinity and affiliation and specified four facets of association (primacy, frequency, duration, and intensity). These facets, if operationalized, would enable us to predict which juveniles were most likely to acquire delinquent and/or criminal patterns of behavior. Simply put, the nature of one's associates is determined by the family into which one is born, by the neighborhood in which one grows up, by the proximity of one's schoolmates to one's neighborhood, by the nature of one's schoolmates even if they are not close by, and so on. Measures of interaction with delinquent vs. non-delinquent companions indicate the probability that the scale will be tipped in one direction rather than another as time goes by. Glaser (1956) added a social psychological component when he spoke of differential identification which, while related to Sutherland's intensity dimension, is really closer to that aspect of explanations referred to by Matza (1969) as signification, i.e., who are the significant others in one's life, delinquents or non-delinquents?

Most recently Akers' (1973) emphasis on social learning models added momentum to the movement away from medical models. It posited delinquency as socially acquired behavior rather than as innate or determined by some inner biological mechanism. This conceptualization of delinquency still does not tell us much about who will become delinquent and who will remain non-delinquent unless we know the social context of learning.

These paragraphs are only a brief introduction to the various social structure/social process theories but are included so that the reader may recognize our social structure/social process theoretical orientation at the outset. What commenced as a prediction study became an attempt to understand the development of delinquency and its limited continuity into criminal careers.

The Wolfgang, Figlio, and Sellin cohort study provided the impetus for us to turn from our earlier social structurally oriented cross-sectional work in Madison and Racine (Voss, 1956; McCaghy, 1962; Turk, 1962, 1964; Shannon, 1963, 1964, 1967; Terry, 1966, 1967a, 1967b) to our first longitudinal cohort research in Racine. Although we have not replicated Wolfgang, Figlio, and Sellin's (1972) longitudinal cohort study of almost 10,000 Philadelphia boys from age 8 to age 18, their major concerns have been close to ours (Petersilia, 1980). When we embarked on the longitudinal birth cohort prediction work, it seemed that we would be remiss not to combine this approach with our prior efforts to incorporate the strength of social structure theory in an effort to account for delinquency and crime in middle-sized cities that were only then developing highly visible ecological indicators of structure.

We have, following the Chicago model, emphasized the nature of subareas in which juveniles are socialized as the social context for learning. Juveniles grow up in a neighborhood, a social or ecological area (and if their parents move about, are likely to do so within similar areas) with more or less distinctive social characteristics, crime and delinquency levels (Mack, 1963; Block, 1979; Roncek, 1981), attitudes toward the police and the juvenile and adult justice systems, and patterns of interaction between juveniles, adults, and representatives of the larger society. Miller's (1958) description of the focal concerns of the lower class culture (trouble, toughness, smartness, excitement, fate, and autonomy) are helpful in understanding how the behavior of lower class youth makes them visible to and in conflict with the law.

Juveniles acquire the attitudes and behaviors prevalent in the type of neighborhood in which they are socialized. How a juvenile is insulated from becoming delinquent while surrounded by delinquent peers must be accounted for by the presence of role models or meaningful others who supplant those in residential or other proximity. As time passes, juvenile misbehavior produces reactions by society, including society's label for the delinquent, as well as a juvenile's own self-definitions and sometimes consequent changes in behavior that are associated with a change from primary to secondary deviation (Welford, 1975; Ferdinand and Luchterhand, 1970; Schur, 1971; Williams and Gold, 1972). This view of delinquency (as a chain of events in a hostile social environment) has been supported by Ferracuti, Dinitz, and Acosta de Brenes (1975) in their Puerto Rican research on juvenile delinquency.

As adults, people no longer find themselves in many types of situations which generate the kinds of misbehavior that earlier resulted in trouble with other adults, particularly the police. In many cases the behaviors which produced trouble have been legalized, i.e., they are no longer status offenses (behaviors which are forbidden for juveniles but allowed for adults). Although there seems to be an element of "maturation" involved in most juvenile careers, we do not view it in a psychological framework but as the acceptance of new statuses and recognition of the availability of social opportunities and alternatives that were not present at an earlier age.

Adolescence is usually followed by a change in outlook and behavior. It is not simply a matter of growing up or settling down and securing work that was previously unavailable. For most young people it is a matter of getting married, assuming various financial responsibilities, and acquiring statuses that obviate the likelihood of contact-generating behavior. Interviews have revealed that respondents had re-evaluated their behavior and had changed their self-concepts. If, however, the worlds of education and work do not facilitate this transition, it is difficult to see how responsible adult behavior can follow the juvenile period.

The Incidence and Prevalence of Delinquency and Crime

In our report on the first stage of this research to the National Institute of Juvenile Justice and Delinquency Prevention, *Assessing* (Shannon, 1980b), two substantive chapters dealt with the ecology of delinquency and crime.[1] Variation in delinquency and crime rates, statistics on both the incidence and prevalence of delinquency and crime in the larger natural areas and other spatial units, and their changing patterns including the changing distribution of both offenses and offenders, served to support Chicago's classical ecological model of delinquency and crime. Racine's twenty-six spatial subareas had varying degrees of physical and demographic homogeneity, delinquency, and crime and provided empirical support for the Chicago cultural deviance theories (social structure) of delinquency and crime. We clearly saw the development of an inner city, interstitial areas, various types of stable residential areas, and then the suburban fringe, all with more or less distinctive land uses and varying demographic characteristics.

There were reasonably systematic declines from the inner city and interstitial areas to the suburban fringe in the incidence and prevalence of delinquency and crime, in the seriousness of offenses, and in the seriousness of delinquent and criminal careers. Seriousness of offenses was determined by the place of police contact on a six-point scale ranging from felonies against the person such as murder and assault to non-offenses consisting of contacts for suspicion, investigation, or information. The concentration of persons with serious offender careers is clearly seen in Maps 2.1, 2.2, and 2.3 where mean grand seriousness scores (number of police contacts by offense seriousness) by place of residence of cohort members are highest in the inner city and interstitial areas as well as in a developing commercial-industrial area on the periphery. The fact that there were differences within spatial subareas and within the five major groupings of areas following the Chicago concentric circle model made it clear, however, that cultural deviance (social structure theory) and the hypotheses derived from it that some subcultures produce different types and rates of delinquency and crime from others, at least as tested with an ecological model, did not completely account for variation in rates of delinquency and crime.

Differences in the incidence and prevalence of delinquency and crime were sharpest between the inner city, interstitial, and then all other areas. This was consistent with what we would expect based on Miller (1958), Cloward and Ohlin (1960), Bordua (1961), Schultz (1962), Short and Strodbeck (1965), Lerman (1968), Wolfgang and Ferracuti (1967), Short (1968), and many others who have recognized but somewhat differently conceptualized the influence of the lower class subculture in generating patterns of delinquency and crime.

An argument could be made that our data lend some support to strain theory (Merton, 1957), strain-subculture theory (Cohen, 1955), opportunity theory (Cloward and Ohlin, 1960), theories which attribute delinquency to the difficulty that persons in lower SES groups have in reaching their immediate life goals because of scarce opportunities for persons in their position.

The relationship of delinquency and crime rates in three birth cohorts to the social organization of the city and its related subcultures does not preclude the importance and validity of non-structural theories. Examination of the data from several social process perspectives indicated that they may also be helpful in accounting for delinquency and crime by explaining the variation in rates (incidence and/or prevalence), even that which occurs *within* subareas. The interview data describing life experiences and attitudes, as we shall later see, provided support for a social control theory, such as Hirschi's bonding theory (1969), that emphasizes attachment to non-delinquent, familial, or other role models. Support was also evident for Lemert's labeling theory (1967) which may be expanded into the delinquent self-label as a consequence of societal reaction to one's behavior or reaction to labels placed on one by persons in positions of either esteem or authority. Rather than rejecting all but one well-conceptualized explanation of delinquency and/or crime, our official police report and interview data suggested that it is a matter of

GRAND SERIOUSNESS SCORES COMPUTER-CONTOURED BASED ON POLICE CONTACTS PER PERSON
WITH CONTINUOUS RESIDENCE BY AREA OF JUVENILE RESIDENCE

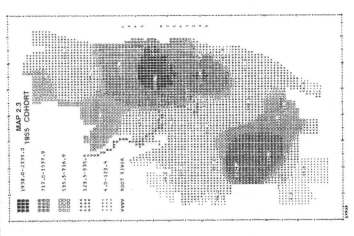

MAP 2.3
1955 COHORT

1938.0-2339.0
717.0-1937.9
535.5-716.9
123.5-535.4
4.0-123.4
ROOT RIVER

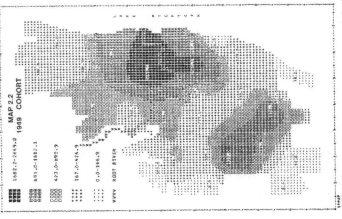

MAP 2.2
1949 COHORT

1882.2-2649.0
891.0-1882.1
427.0-895.9
167.0-426.9
0.0-166.9
ROOT RIVER

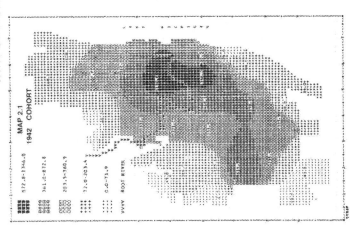

MAP 2.1
1942 COHORT

572.8-1346.0
361.0-822.8
203.5-360.9
72.0-203.4
0.0-71.9
ROOT RIVER

numerous theories playing a part in accounting for all delinquency and crime.

As the story unfolded in *Assessing*, it became clearer and clearer that, although there was a concentration of delinquency and crime in the inner city and interstitial areas and among multiple offenders who resided there, delinquency and crime were also present throughout the city. The widespread prevalence of police contacts and referrals called for an integrated theory of delinquency which would account for not only differences in delinquency and crime produced by structural differences, the organization of society which produced systematic spatial variation, but for differences within areas as well. These differences might be based on social bonds, containment, or the act of apprehension which would serve as the first step toward a delinquent label.

As the preliminary analyses were completed, chapter by chapter, we saw how even though continuity in delinquent and criminal careers was greatest in the inner city and interstitial areas, it too varied within areas. We had not, of course, overlooked the demographic characteristics of cohort juveniles, i.e., race/ethnicity and sex, but had accepted them as variables traditionally associated with delinquency, correlated but not explanatory. They would not be really useful in understanding the processes by which delinquent and criminal behavior are acquired, unless associated with different life experiences or when antecedent effects turned out to vary by race/ethnicity or sex.

All of this pointed to the need for an interviewing strategy to determine which aspects of structure, process, and institutional involvement were most important in accounting for differences in the incidence and prevalence of delinquency and crime and continuation in either or both. The official police contact and referral data would only take us so far.

Demographic Variation

As it turned out, comparing age, race/ethnic, and sex trends was an important element of the analysis. Cohort members not only had more frequent police contacts at the age of 16 or 17 but these contacts were, on the average, for more serious offenses (felony-level Index offenses or Part I), as shown in Diagram 2.1. Contacts for auto-related offenses, considered less serious, made up a greater proportion of each cohort's contacts as the years went by. Police contact rates for juvenile males remained universally higher than those for females, whether White, Black, or Chicano. Rates for Blacks and Chicanos remained higher than for Whites. Rates for females showed a greater increase from cohort to cohort than did those for males. The same may be said almost without

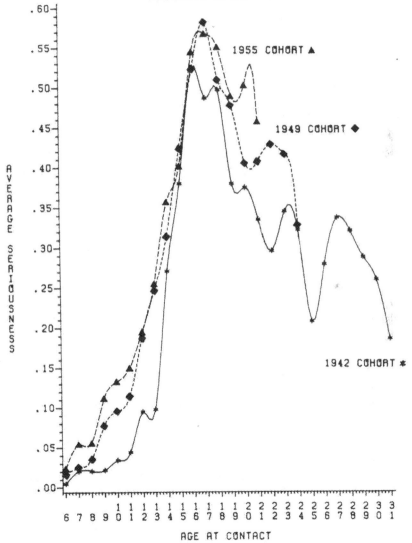

DIAGRAM 2.1

AVERAGE SERIOUSNESS OF POLICE CONTACTS

FOR COHORT AT AGE

exception for offense seriousness, as indicated by the proportion of contacts which were Part I or Index offenses. The upward trend for females was not as clear-cut for the 18 through 20 or 21 and older age periods. As was true of measures of incidence and seriousness, there was a disproportional rise in prevalence among females but prevalence still remained lower among females.

These findings, rather than supporting the position that women's liberation and economic emancipation had led to a higher and differently constructed crime rate (Austin, 1982), were more supportive of the position that although females do commit most of the offenses that males commit (to a lesser extent) female increases have not been for offenses which are destructive or a threat to society but for offenses that have traditionally been female offenses, such as theft (Giallombardo, 1980; Steffensmeier and Steffensmeier, 1980; and Weis, 1976). Giallombardo's observation of Uniform Crime Report data from 1960 to 1976, for example, indicated that the gap between male and female juveniles had narrowed to a greater degree than it had for male and female adults, but the contribution of females, juvenile or adult, to the total still remained small.

A large part of *Assessing* was devoted to a statistical description of differences in rates of continuity and discontinuity by cohort and sex, first on a contact by contact and then on an age period by age period basis. All of this served to show us that most members of each cohort would have relatively short careers, females shorter than males.

Surprising to many was the fact that sizeable proportions of those who had no police contacts as juveniles did so as adults, 15% for the 1955 Cohort males in their first three years as adults (18-20) whether they lived in the inner city and interstitial areas or in outlying areas. Although juvenile to adult continuity was not consistently greater for males from the inner city and interstitial areas than from other areas, it was for females.

Perhaps even more surprising was our inability to predict from juvenile records much more efficiently than from the modal category of the marginals (most frequently appearing) who would have police contacts as adults, much less how many contacts or how serious the reason for contact (Shannon, 1985). Although it is obvious that persons from the inner city and interstitial areas with the most serious continuous careers had the greatest continuity in adult careers, there are also a variety of extra-legal factors which play a part in continuity just as neither delinquency nor crime is usually generated simply by chance encounters. It is the explication of this which becomes so difficult when only the official records are available.

This difficulty was further highlighted when the disposition of police contacts was described, for here we found variation in referral rates by race/ethnicity and sex even when offense seriousness was controlled. It is not possible to determine how much of this could be accounted for by a combination of differences in place of residence and by the fact that labeling is not difficult in a community of 100,000. The statistics on police contacts, referrals, and institutionalization indicated, however, that step by step the inner city Black was more likely to reach an institution than was an inner city White counterpart. This finding is consistent with a lengthy literature on dispositions (Green, 1970; Thornberry, 1973; Lizotte, 1978; Bernstein, Kelly, and Doyle, 1977; Tittle, Villemez, and Smith, 1978; Petersilia, 1983; Zatz, 1984; and Welch, Spohn, and Gruhl, 1985).

Not only were dispositions affected by extra-legal factors, perhaps with justification as perceived by the judge, but the more severely juveniles were sanctioned, the more serious was their behavior in the period thereafter. Since institutionalization was the severest sanction, we have tended to interpret this as support for differential association, i.e., as delinquents were placed in close proximity, they influenced each other even more than when growing up in the same neighborhoods.

There is also evidence that institutionalized delinquents returned upon release to their old neighborhoods and old friends and associates, and were soon involved in the same or more serious activity. For even those who had left the institution with the firmest resolve to become law-abiding, the chance of continued resolution would be small in such a social environment. Furthermore, in a series of multivariate analyses (path analyses) with controls for cohort and sex, where it could be said that all other things were equal, it was shown that juvenile referrals and sanctions had little or no deterrent effect on offense seriousness after the age of 18. Even more specifically, the agencies of social control, almost without exception, did not play even a moderate role in bringing about a decrease in the seriousness of adult police contacts; if anything, they seemed to promote adult seriousness. The impact of labeling cohort members as they experienced contact with the justice system is difficult to ascertain.

What the Interview Data Added

Whether or not delinquent youth continue or discontinue their misbehavior, they are influenced by the actions of persons in authority and by their perceptions of decision-makers in the justice system. Likewise, the judge is influenced by the juvenile's cumulative record of misbehavior and by his/her perception of what other decision-makers have done with the juvenile in similar cases. In shaping the interview schedule we utilized a perspective that took into consideration feedback from juveniles to system decision-makers and back again to the juveniles. We hoped to enhance our understanding of juvenile misbehavior and its continuation or discontinuation by relating interview data to the chains of official events obtained from our records.

The value of self-reports as a supplement to official police contact and referral data has been argued since the early Short and Nye (1957) reports (Hindelang, Hirschi, and Weis, 1979 and 1981). There has also been an extensive literature on race and class differences in self-reports vs. official data (Elliott and Ageton, 1980; Young, 1980; Adler, 1975) but we shall simply say that many arguable differences may be reconciled by examining the instruments and samples utilized.

In Shannon (1980b), self-report data revealed that 95.4% of the 1942 Cohort males and 93.9% of the 1949 Cohort males stated that they had either been stopped by the police or had done things for which they could have been stopped (see Table 2.1). However, only 63.8% of the 95.4% and 71.2% of the 93.9% actually showed up in the police records for a police contact before reaching 18.

The group stopped by the police who also stated that they didn't do other things for which they could have been stopped contained 61.8% and 52.4% with police records. And, of course, about 30% to 40% of those who said that they had not been stopped by the police appeared in the police records as having been stopped. Put more simply, in the 1949 Cohort 54.8% of the males admitted police contacts before 18 and had a police record, 13% admitted no police contacts and had no record, 24.3% who thought that they had a police contact had none, and 7.4% had a record but admitted no police contacts. There were some differences by race/ethnicity but the greatest difference was between sexes within race/ethnic groups.

While some may perceive these responses as deception or error, they may also be explained in other ways as well, e.g., the police did not fill out a report or respondents did not perceive their contact with the police as worth mentioning because it was in the suspicion, information, investigation category. Whatever, this is why we tend to agree with those who see both official and self-report data as valuable and complementary.

Understanding Institutional Effects

The school may be perceived within a structural framework (Polk and Schafer, 1972) as a primary cause of delinquency or in a social process

TABLE 2.1   PERCENT OF THE 1942 AND 1949 COHORTS INTERVIEWED WHO ADMITTED MISBEHAVIOR
BEFORE THE AGE OF 18 (DETECTED AND UNDETECTED), BY SEX AND COHORT

	1942			1949		
	M	F	T	M	F	T
Stopped by police; did things	62.3	21.6	40.4	65.3	28.2	46.8
Stopped by police; didn't do things	13.9	11.9	12.8	12.3	13.4	12.8
Not stopped by police; did things	19.2	31.3	25.7	16.2	29.6	22.9
Not stopped; didn't do things	4.6	35.2	21.1	6.1	28.9	17.5
	100.0	100.0	100.0	99.9	100.1	100.0
Either stopped or did things	95.4	64.8	78.9	93.9	71.1	82.5
N =	151	176	327	277	277	554

(lack of bond to the school) framework. It can be thought of as providing external containment, as an agency of social control, and as a place in which juveniles are labeled and, once labeled (by school officials), fulfill the prophecy (Kelly, 1976).

Those interviewed from either cohort who had graduated from high school had lower official seriousness scores than those who had not graduated, suggesting that those who had difficulty achieving in the school system had higher offense seriousness scores. This finding was consistent with the Wolfgang, Figlio, and Sellin (1972) and most other research relating school performance to delinquency (Jensen, 1976; Jensen and Rojek, 1980). The only major discrepancy was that those who had been expelled who had a negative attitude toward school had lower seriousness scores than did others after the age of 18. It would seem that the latter fit into one of the patterns described by Elliott and Voss (1974), that is, a decline in delinquency after leaving school. We have been reluctant to push these findings, however, because the number who failed to receive a diploma became quite small in some cells when controls for sex and attitude toward school were introduced.

Those respondents who worked before age 18 were more likely to have had higher offense rates and higher seriousness scores than those who had not worked. Whether it was more money in their pockets and thus an opportunity for wider experiences or the associations that they made in the world of work, early work resulted in a ratio of more frequent and more serious contacts after commencing work than before work, the earlier that work commenced. These differences were less consistent for females, however. There is also the possibility that work reduced the bond to school and that drop-out followed. The very complexity of accounting for delinquency and crime makes it difficult to set up a test which will reject a set of theories and leave one as the most viable explanation.

Questions on occupational level and income of cohort respondents and on occupational level and regularity of employment of their parents gave further but not strong support to strain theory, the idea that delinquency is generated by the frustration experienced by those unable to achieve success through legitimate procedures, depending on how one interpret the findings. The data could also be interpreted as giving even more support to cultural deviance, the idea that an all-pervasive subculture of delinquency supersedes the culture of the larger society. Most of the differences in offense seriousness that were correlated with variable representing experiences in the world of work were found with consistency for only the Black males, a group for whom this would have been predicted by either strain or cultural deviance theories. This was during a period when, at the same time that the minority group population was struggling for economic absorption, many heavy industries were closing their doors.

Another set of variables includes family type during the juvenile period and parents' marital status, variables suggested by social structure and social process theory. There has been a controversy among sociologists (Wilkinson, 1974) on the impact of the broken home that commenced at the turn of the century and was continued into the 1930s by Gillin (1933) and Shaw and McKay (1931). A period of relatively little interest followed until the 1950s. Renewed attention did not, however, culminate in an affirmation of family effects on delinquency (Chilton and Markle, 1972). We, as did Toby (1957), found the issue compounded by male/female differences in juveniles' reactions to the broken home. The impact of both parents not being present in the home was small but greater for females than males.

Leaving home at an early age was followed by higher average numbers of contacts and higher offense seriousness rates. Age at marriage for members of the 1942 and 1949 Cohorts did not have a consistent relationship to number and seriousness of police contacts for males but early marriage was followed by an increase in offenses for females in both cohorts.

A more definitive exposition of how the numerous interview variables lent support to or tended to reject social structure and social process theories must await the multivariate analyses in a later chapter. These analyses will lead to our tentative account of how delinquency and crime develop and continue, an account which should be helpful to the development of a more general theory of delinquency.

Delinquents' Perceptions of Their Behavior

Perusal of the data often suggests very simple explanations for a large proportion of either self-reported or officially recorded delinquent behavior. Our own interview data indicate that over 50% of all police contacts, in the words of the respondents, took place for fun, involved the use of unstructured time, were unintentional, or the respondent just happened to be there. Of those misbehaviors which they reported but which did not result in police contacts, about one-third were liquor violations.

Most males admitted participation in behavior that either got them into trouble or could have done so. About 40% said that what they had done was their own idea; 85% to 90% were with persons they usually ran around with. Less than 20% said that they had done what they did while alone. Of the total events described by respondents, over 70% of each cohort attributed their behavior to the desire for fun, use of unstructured time, and peer influences. Between 50% and 60% said that they later stopped doing these things because they had changed their self-concept, values, or had reassessed their behavior.

That about 70% of the respondents in each cohort said that their parents had a positive influence on their decisions, attitudes, and/or behavior provided support for Hirschi's social control theory (bonding). If the ratio of positive to negative influences is considered, students at school provided the greatest (retrospectively) negative influences. Here the Jessors' (1977) conception of a person's perceived environment consisting of a distal and proximal structure is useful. The proximal structure refers to role models found around the juvenile, in the neighborhood, in the school, and at work, while the more remote distal structure refers to a person's perception of support and controls from friends and parents. If the latter appear to be in disagreement, particularly when juveniles are most susceptible to having police contacts, the juvenile is more likely to engage in problem behavior.

The Racine interview data indicated that respondents' perceptions of their friends' delinquent/non-delinquent concept of them had a slightly higher correlation with respondents' self-reported seriousness than did their reported perception of teachers and parents about themselves. Thus, although friends obviously knew about their behavior, respondents did not think that their friends were very much concerned about it.

All of this lends support to explanations revolving around the theme of delinquency and relatively uncontrolled adolescence, long considered a period of crisis, perhaps exaggerated for some, but for most a stage in the process of socialization. During this period youth are probably at the

peak of their alertness, about as inventive as they will ever be in some
respects, but still with controls imposed by adults who have forgotten their
own search for excitement or at least do not relate it to the new forms that
are disturbing and unfamiliar to them. Actually, most juveniles who
become involved in behavior which makes up the bulk of the incidents to
which we have referred are relatively well adjusted and are not in a state
of crisis or anxiety. Part of what juveniles do may be viewed as a
struggle to break from their childhood cocoons, just as each generation
before them has done. Although some juveniles may be engaged in
potentially harmful activities, this does not mean that it is necessary to
explain juvenile misbehavior in such a convoluted fashion as have some
behavioral or social scientists (Reiss, 1960).

We have hesitated to bring our own attitudinal data into the argument
because it is so difficult to place retrospective data in an
antecedent/consequence framework, e.g., attitudes toward police vs.
offense seriousness scales, even when time periods are supplied for
responses to the attitudinal questions. The more serious one's record, the
more negative one's attitude toward the police and perhaps the reverse.

Turning back to questions which are less troublesome, aside from the
memory problem, those who had friends in trouble with the police had
higher seriousness scores than those who did not, a relationship supportive
of Sutherland's differential association hypothesis. Even more supportive
was the fact that those who had friends in trouble with the police as
juveniles and as adults had even higher offense seriousness scores as
adults than did those who had only juvenile friends in trouble with the
police as juveniles. These relationships also play a part in integrated
theories such as those set forth by Weis and Sederstrom (1981) and
Elliott, Huizinga, and Ageton (1985).

Findings from the Multivariate Analysis

Separate multivariate analyses were conducted for the males and
females of each interviewed cohort, regressing official and self-report
seriousness scores for the juvenile and adult periods on race/ethnic and
ecological variables as well as on a multitude of other interview
variables. There was an effort to determine which variables had the
greatest explanatory value and which of the diverse theories of
delinquency and crime would receive some support from these analyses.

Among the more important effects on juvenile seriousness were area of
residence, race, school dropout, and having had friends in trouble with the
police. Cultural deviance and the subculture of poverty, as represented
by place of residence, continued to receive support when all other

variables were held constant. In other words, the findings were not inconsistent with what one would expect from the positions set forth over the years by Shaw and McKay, Merton, Miller, Cohen, and others. These data, however, are not specific to one rather than another cultural deviance theory. Clearly, more explicit tests of these hypotheses would be necessary were our goal (as maybe it should be) to reject, one by one, these competing theories of delinquent behavior.

Perhaps even more difficult is the interpretation of school dropout. It takes relatively little imagination to see dropout as consistent with social structure theory, social process theory, labeling theory, or social conflict theory. Only a set of questions designed to specify the nature of the interaction between students, peers, teachers, and meaningful others in their lives, questions which distinguish between the nature of interaction specific to each theory, would give us a definitive answer.

As we concluded *Assessing*, we indicated that part of the problem might be that delinquency and crime had been conceptualized as social problems rather than as sociological problems, that is, behaviors that should be explained at a level which transcends the influence of historical events which make one ten-year time period different from another or events which make one cohort different from another. The problem that we have is one of overcoming tangentially-related phenomena which overshadow the social (sociological) causes of delinquency and crime. For example, only 37.3% of the official and 34.9% of the 1949 Cohort males' self-reported juvenile offense seriousness was accounted for at the individual level analyses. While more adult seriousness was accounted for, 52.4% and 44.9%, the variables which we selected, guided by contemporary theory, did not account for more than about 50% of the adult crime. Moreover, as it turned out, juvenile seriousness was the most powerful determinant of adult seriousness.

All of this made us think about some of our original concerns again, e.g., the measures that we had used. Since place of residence was an independent variable which had significant effects on delinquency and crime, even with spatial units which had a degree of internal heterogeneity (as observed from examination of block data) and the characteristics of spatial areas were changing over time, might it not be wise to look into the changing ecology of the city rather than just the ecology of the city and note its relationship to changing patterns of delinquency and crime?

Note

1. *Assessing the Relationship of Adult Criminal Careers to Juvenile Careers* (Shannon, 1980b), National Institute of Juvenile Justice and Delinquency Prevention, Grant Number 76-JN-99-0008, 76-JN-99-1005, 79-JN-99-0019, and 79-JN-AX-0010. The first and second stages of the research have been described most recently in Lyle W. Shannon, *Criminal Career Continuity: Its Social Context*. New York: Human Sciences Press, 1988.

Chapter 3

THE RELATIONSHIP OF JUVENILE DELINQUENCY AND ADULT CRIME TO THE CHANGING CITY STRUCTURE

The Theoretical and Empirical Problem

Rather than being satisfied with the existence of a relationship between patterns of delinquency and crime and land use, population density, housing quality, etc. (indicators of a different way of life), we added a dynamic aspect to the research by examining the relationship of change in delinquency/crime to change in social and ecological structure. Which appeared first? Did structure determine delinquency and crime rates or did the latter determine structure? Did delinquency/crime increase with the growth of deteriorated areas or did the growth of deteriorated areas enlarge the boundaries of high delinquency and crime areas? Or were delinquency and crime rates and changes in land use/life style fairly independent phenomena which occurred as the city grew and developed?

In earlier periods sociologists considered the growth of deteriorated and overcrowded housing, abandoned buildings, commercial-industrial establishments, numerous taverns, and a population that had neither been absorbed into the economy nor integrated into the broader social structure of the community to be distinctive of interstitial or transitional areas. These areas had long been productive of delinquency and crime and would continue to be so as long as they and their residents were unchanged.

When public housing replaced rat-infested dwellings, the resident population sometimes changed as well (the poorest were replaced by those who could meet minimal income requirements) or they stayed but did not change, i.e., they were neither absorbed nor integrated, and a high-rise slum was born. That was, of course, not the situation in Racine because it had not had public housing, not that it didn't need some. The point is that whether we describe change in the old fashioned way with deterioration and decay either preceding or following increasing delinquency and crime, both people and the physical structure of Racine had changed.

Behind all of this we would not forget that such changes as rapidly growing automobile registrations and declining use of public transportation had influenced offender residence patterns vs. where offenses were committed. Not only that, but the structured movement that had been set up by street cars and then buses changed as the automobile provided more direct access to all areas, although access was still limited by sprawling industrial complexes or parks and public use areas as well as by rivers and ravines. Coupled with this has been a pattern of peripheral development which placed new targets for delinquency and crime at intervals along and at the end of major arterials so that areas once too distant became within reach of or even at the doorstep of offenders (Bursik and Webb, 1982).

We also considered how a developing or declining economy influenced physical and structural changes in areas and stimulated or retarded population growth and movement. How these changes facilitated or impeded the absorption of youth into the economy and the larger society must be understood if we are to even begin to explain changing patterns of delinquency and crime. Having introduced these basic considerations, it is not difficult to see how an ecological approach, basically a social structure explanation of patterns of delinquency and crime, led us to simultaneously think about social processes and social conflict (Clark and Wenninger, 1962; Johnstone, 1978).

In the second stage of the research our first goal was to determine if spatial units existed or could be constructed that would reduce the heterogeneity that had been found within the five major areas of Racine and even within some subareas.[1] Eliminating heterogeneity completely would not be possible but surely the people in a single block are more alike than are the people in a square mile of Racine; city blocks became our building blocks for the construction of relatively homogeneous neighborhoods.

The Problem of Homogeneous Spatial Units

Our concern about homogeneous spatial units and the differences in findings that might be derived from the twenty-six subareas and five major natural areas vs. fifteen census tracts, twenty police grid areas, and sixty-five neighborhoods (spatial units available for analysis) led to the utilization of twenty-eight different land use, housing characteristics, and population variables in characterizing each spatial unit in each spatial system for 1950, 1960, 1970, and 1980. For example, the inner city and transitional areas decreased in population between 1950 and 1980 while all peripheral, high socioeconomic status areas increased in population during this period. The residents of inner city neighborhoods had low mean incomes and low household possessions scale sores and there was a high percentage of Blacks and female heads of household, a contrast to the usually medium or high income and high household possessions scale scores and low percentage of Blacks and female-headed households in other areas of the city. The inner city areas were predominantly business, commercial, and manufacturing and had high target densities compared with peripheral areas. In the latter, residential housing quality was high or medium while that in the inner city was low. Perhaps most important, the inner city and transitional areas had what has been considered to be delinquency and crime producing characteristics while all but on one of the peripheral residential areas were low in this respect.

In another detailed examination of Racine's areas, we found that the occupational level of one's associates, satisfaction with pay, antecedent handicaps, level of education, anticipated level of education for children, level of social participation, and world view varied sharply between inner city and transitional areas and those which were high socioeconomic status areas on the periphery of the city. In sum, interview data obtained from samples of the population from twenty-six subareas indicated that they markedly varied from the inner city to the periphery.

Each spatial unit was categorized according to each system as: the Inner City, Interstitial or Transitional areas, Stable or Middle Class Residential areas, and Peripheral Middle and High SES areas. Heterogeneity was greatest within Police Grids and homogeneity was greatest within neighborhoods. A test of cultural deviance theory or any other theory based on variables with spatially varying units produces somewhat different answers depending on the spatial system utilized. This problem is not new to sociologists who have conducted research within an ecological framework (Schmid and MacCannel, 1955).

Another difficulty in making any definitive test of the relationship of social structure change (ecology) to rates of delinquency and crime is that, no matter which spatial system is utilized, year to year delinquency and crime rates vary within spatial units. Sometimes rates vary in a very spectacular manner, more in one spatial unit than another and particularly in the areas outside the inner city and transitional area. This, of course, means that there is considerable change from year to year within the same kinds of subcultural areas. Any rate for a given time period is at most some measure of cultural tendency, the mean or median of that period for that area. One might say that fluctuations about the mean must be accounted for by other independent variables which are crucial elements in some period/event driven theory of changing rates of delinquent and/or criminal behavior. This is a problem whether we are discussing offenses committed by residents of an area or offenses which occurred in the area.

Keeping all of this in mind, we constructed a series of tables in which the target density, commercial/industrial composition, residential vacancies, and housing quality scores of each census tract were shown for 1950, 1960, and 1970. Change was shown for each variable from period to period and was related to arrests by residence and by place of offense. Although there were several patterns of arrest and offense rates and changes in rates within each group of census tracts, it was also evident that the cycle of deterioration and movement outward from the inner city tracts was followed by increasing delinquency and crime. This increase in turn was followed by further deterioration and departure of people and targets from the area, a finding consistent with that for the thirty-two largest U.S. cities for approximately the same period (Skogman, 1977). Police grid areas, even more heterogeneous than census tracts, produced a less consistent pattern of change overall but again showed how the inner city differed in structure, offense rates, and changing offense rates from other groups of grids.

A series of regression analyses of arrest rates also showed that, although characteristics of census tracts appear to be powerful determinants of arrest rates, change in tract characteristics from 1950 to 1960 to 1970 had little effect on change in arrest rates and change in arrest rates had little effect on tract characteristics. The same kind of analysis with police grids had generated such a different set of change relationships that we concluded that neither tracts nor grids had produced a definitive test of the hypothesis.

Nevertheless, when the cohort data were analyzed within each of the spatial system models, higher rates of contacts, higher offense seriousness, higher rates of referrals, and higher severity of sanctions were consistently found in the inner city (whether based on all cohort members or only those with police contacts for the 1950s, the 1960s, and the 1970s), with rates declining toward the peripheral areas. Although this decline did not have the high degree of regularity that would be expected as that found zone by zone following the Chicago model, inner city vs. other delinquency and crime rates were always significantly different and became more pronounced from decade to decade.

Furthermore, one would not expect quite so much regularity in the decline from the inner city to peripheral areas within any spatial system for a city of 100,000 which did not have quite such distinctive spatial differences as found in older smokestack cities. That these differences were developing could be seen in any series of maps based on cohorts or ten-year periods commencing in the 1950s. The differences became particularly notable when various offense rates and neighborhood land use, housing, or demographic characteristics were shown in three-dimensional maps by ten-year periods or by cohorts. (See Maps 3.1 to 3.4 for examples of target and minority group density and Maps 3.5 and 3.7 for examples of neighborhood variation in the incidence of police contacts, mean offense seriousness, and mean referral rates.) While in-area contact rates and by place of residence rates were not congruent, it became apparent that inner city and some interstitial neighborhoods were developing enduring patterns of delinquency and crime.

Adding a Dynamic Model

We also developed a number of dynamic models which represented expected cohort and age changes in number and seriousness of offenses, frequency of referral, and severity of sanctions. The changes which would be expected in a table with four age categories for each of the three cohorts were specified; the model could be further complicated by specifying the time periods for each cohort and age group (see Table 3.1). Lab and Doerner (1985) have shown that age, period, and cohort effects are present in the 1942 and 1949 Cohorts for males but that influences with the female members of the cohorts vary depending upon offense types. The model also specified that each of the twelve cells in an inner city area would have high police contact, referral, and sanctions rates (for each cohort and each age period) and that a high SES, peripheral neighborhood would have low rates for each of the twelve cells. There were eleven different patterns representing the transition of spacial unit rates through time and age of cohort members plus a no-discernible-pattern category.

TABLE 3.1   RELATIONSHIP OF TIME PERIODS TO COHORTS AND AGE GROUPS WITHIN YEARS COVERED BY POLICE CONTACT DATA

Cohort	Ages 6-10	Ages 11-14	Ages 15-17	Ages 18-20
1955	1960-69 1961	1960-69	1970+	1970+ 1971
1949	1950-59 1955	1960-69	1960-69	1970+ 1974
1942	1950-59 1948	1950-59	1950-59	1960-69 1974

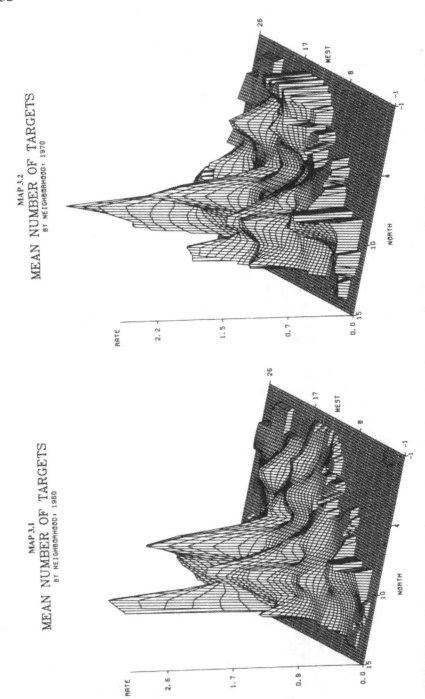

MAP 3.2
MEAN NUMBER OF TARGETS
BY NEIGHBORHOOD: 1970

MAP 3.1
MEAN NUMBER OF TARGETS
BY NEIGHBORHOOD: 1960

33

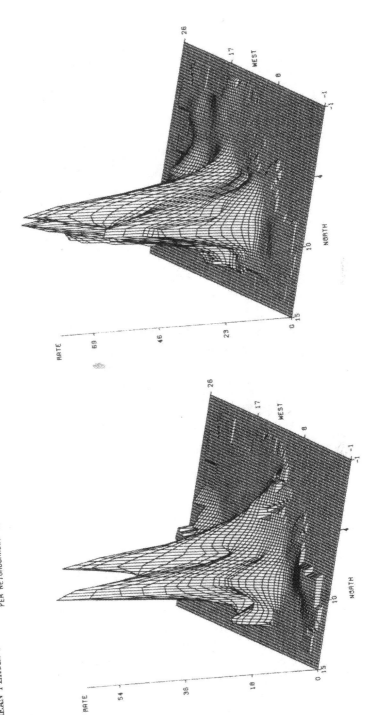

MAP 3.3
MEAN PERCENT OCCUPIED DWELLING UNITS OCCUPIED BY BLACKS
PER NEIGHBORHOOD--1960

MAP 3.4
MEAN PERCENT OCCUPIED DWELLING UNITS OCCUPIED BY BLACKS
PER NEIGHBORHOOD--1970

MAP 3.5
CONTACTS PER 100 PERSONS BY NEIGHBORHOOD—1970'S
BY NEIGHBORHOOD OF CONTACT

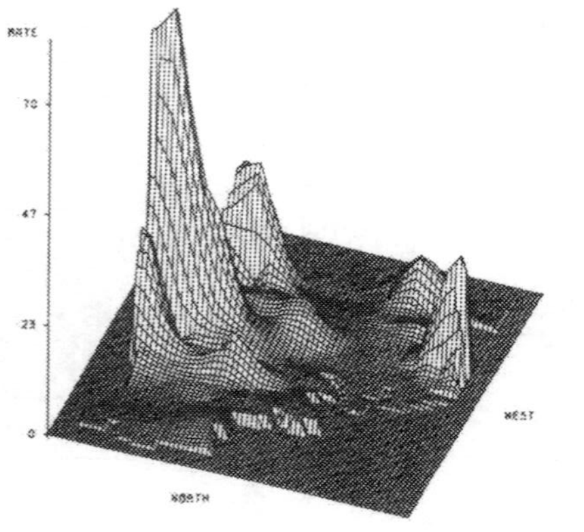

RATE BASED ON COHORT MEMBERS IN NEIGHBORHOOD

MAP 3.6
MEAN SERIOUSNESS SCORES BY NEIGHBORHOOD—1970'S
BY NEIGHBORHOOD OF RESIDENCE

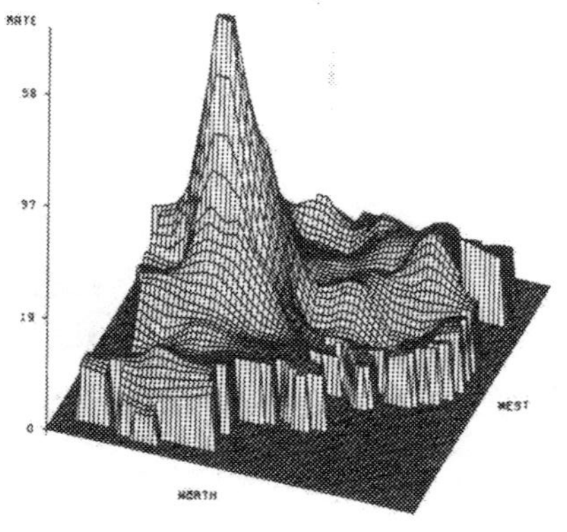

BASED ON COHORT MEMBERS IN NEIGHBORHOOD WITH CONTACTS

MAP 3.7
MEAN NUMBER OF REFERRALS BY NEIGHBORHOOD—1970'S
BY NEIGHBORHOOD OF RESIDENCE

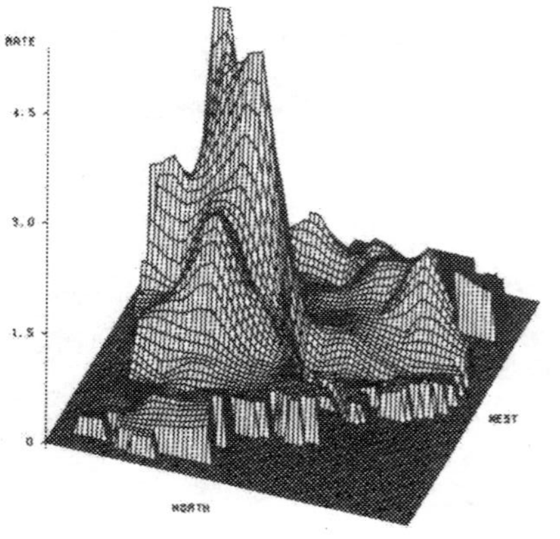

BASED ON COHORT MEMBERS IN NEIGHBORHOOD

One way to characterize age and cohort variation by areas within each spatial system is to consider how the statistics for each area differ from the statistics in Table 3.2. In the first segment of the table one can see how the prevalence of police contacts (percent of the cohort with police contacts) increased with age (for the 1949 and 1955 Cohorts) and by cohort (less systematically). The average number of contacts per person in the cohort (incidence) and average number of contacts by persons with contacts (Shannon, 1982) are shown in the next two segments of the table. We arbitrarily decided that variation by 10% or more from the mean (average number of contacts per person in cohort) would categorize an area as high or low; values within 10% of the mean would be considered the middle category.

We would also expect rates for the inner city areas to be higher on each measure of delinquency for each cohort and each age group. Rates in the interstitial and transitional areas should become higher cohort by cohort and show an age group transformation following a different pattern from that for the city as a whole and a markedly different transformation from that shown for stable residential areas. For the transitional areas we constructed one model for late or nearly complete transition and another model for the early or beginning stages of transition to higher rates. There were a variety of other transitional types to represent high SES areas as well as stable areas in the city which had only cohort change or age group change as a part of their patterned differences.

The complexity of our expectations was also increased by the fact that persons at a given age in one cohort may have resided in the area when it had somewhat different characteristics from that which it had when persons from another cohort resided there. This involves the element of time period change and compounds the difficulty of making comparisons between cohorts for persons aged 11 through 14 in the 1942 and 1949 Cohorts but does not affect comparisons for the 11 through 14 age group between the 1949 and 1955 Cohorts. Comparison of the age group 15 through 17 for the three cohorts is most difficult because this group is in a different time period in each cohort.

Cohort, Age, Time Period, and Spatial Variation in the Prevalence and Incidence of Police Contacts

A lengthy analysis of age, time period, and cohort effects on the prevalence and incidence of police contacts and their spatial pattern for each of the systems provided some evidence of contact rate change consistent with the demographic and classical ecological (Chicago) model of changing delinquency and crime rates. All but two of the thirteen inner

TABLE 3.2   MEASURES OF CONTACT FREQUENCY BY AGE GROUP AND COHORT

	Percent of Cohort with Police Contacts			
Cohort	Ages 6-10	Ages 11-14	Ages 15-17	Ages 18-20
1955	13.6	25.1	40.8	41.2
1949	9.1	26.6	42.3	43.4
1942	3.7	16.3	38.3	35.7

	Average Number of Contacts Per Person in Cohort			
Cohort	Ages 6-10	Ages 11-14	Ages 15-17	Ages 18-20
1955	.27	.91	1.45	1.28
1949	.16	.64	1.41	1.31
1942	.05	.31	1.16	1.09

	Average Number of Contacts by Persons with Contacts			
Cohort	Ages 6-10	Ages 11-14	Ages 15-17	Ages 18-20
1955	2.0	3.6	3.6	3.1
1949	1.8	2.4	3.3	3.0
1942	1.3	1.9	3.0	3.1

city areas with persons from each of the cohorts were found to have high and increasing offense rates or the transitional patterns of increasingly high offense rates. Seven of the ten interstitial neighborhoods could be placed in one of the transitional patterns. One of those which could not was the university area and another had some elements of cohort transition but did not fit the pattern sufficiently well.

Cohort, Age, Time Period, and Spatial Variation in Offense Seriousness

Age group and average cohort offense seriousness (reasons for police contacts) trends for the entire city are shown in Table 3.3. The mean seriousness scores for each cohort and age group were determined for each area in each spatial system and are again characterized as high, medium, or low, depending on the direction they fell from 10% of the mean of the city for that group. Each set of spatial units' pattern of highs, mediums, and lows was in turn characterized according to the models.

We have previously referred to the problem of heterogeneity within spatial systems and its effect on statistics that are assumed to be representative of characteristics and process in an area. Therefore, rather than describing the outcome for each of the spatial systems, we shall turn to the neighborhoods.

All but three of the thirteen inner city neighborhoods had either high seriousness score patterns or appeared to be in transition. Seven of the ten neighborhoods which we had considered in transition for which there were sufficient residents from the cohorts to produce a reliable statistic were in transition to a high seriousness pattern.

We again concluded that the relative homogeneity of neighborhoods facilitates the delineation of areas in which persons reside whose contacts with the police are for more serious reasons, even if the patterns of transition which we proposed do not characterize the areas as neatly as hypothesized. Whatever their patterns of seriousness, there were few neighborhoods within the inner city and transitional areas with many low mean seriousness scores in the age group/cohort segments of their pattern and few middle and high SES neighborhoods with many high mean seriousness scores in their patterns.

Although mean cohort seriousness and seriousness by age group scores followed a gradual transition that is consistent with other findings, the mean offense seriousness pattern *among only those who had had contacts with the police* did not produce such a neat pattern. This was consistent with our earlier findings that seriousness of reasons for police contacts

TABLE 3.3   MEASURES OF CONTACT SERIOUSNESS BY AGE GROUP AND COHORT

	Average Seriousness of Contacts Per Person in Cohort			
Cohort	Ages 6-10	Ages 11-14	Ages 15-17	Ages 18-20
1955	.69	2.64	4.21	3.83
1949	.44	1.65	3.54	3.18
1942	.14	.84	2.84	2.60

	Average Seriousness of Contacts by Persons with Contacts			
Cohort	Ages 6-10	Ages 11-14	Ages 15-17	Ages 18-20
1955	3.4	10.0	10.3	9.3
1949	4.8	6.2	8.4	7.3
1942	3.7	5.2	7.4	7.3

methodically increases through each age group beyond the juvenile perio
for relatively few persons. Some areas were characterized in the sam
way following both procedures but others were different depending o
whether the entire cohort or only those with police contacts wer
considered. This is part of the problem of deciding which measure, tha
for the entire cohort or that for persons with police contacts, best capture
the phenomenon in which one is interested. In most cases, however, w
are concerned about the cohort or a segment thereof rather than with onl
those cohort members who had had police contacts.

Cohort, Age, Time Period, and Spatial Variation in the Prevalence and Incidence of Police Referrals

Once a contact with the police has occurred, one of several things ma
happen to the juvenile or adult. These outcomes depend on th
seriousness of the reason for the contact, the area of the community, th
characteristics of the alleged offender, including demeanor at the time o
contact, the reason that the officer made the contact, i.e., did the office
see the actor do it or was the officer answering a complaint that had bee
communicated from the police station, the characteristics of th

complainant if known to the officer, and the time of day or night. The general policy of the police department on street-level handling rather than referral, the officer's receptivity to departmental policy, and/or, of course, the attitude of the officer toward miscreants encountered on patrol may also influence the outcome.

Our concern, however, was with whether or not those who resided in the inner city and interstitial areas were more likely to be referred than were those who resided in other areas and with whether or not this pattern was changing. We are also concerned about the average number of referrals per person in each area and the average number of referrals for those who had had at least one referral. Since persons living in those areas in which a larger proportion of the cohort had police contacts and in which the mean number of police contacts was high had a greater probability of referral, these statistics should result in separation of the inner city and transitional areas even more clearly than did contacts and seriousness scores.

The percent of those who had been referred in Racine and the mean number of referrals for persons with referrals by age group and cohort indicated that three of the four inner city natural areas were consistently above the other areas on every measure of referrals, followed by the transitional areas. Only one of the other natural areas, a stable residential area, had a pattern of referral statistics which suggested that it was in transition in this respect. In fact, most had relatively low rates for all cohorts in most age groups.

Because referral statistics involve diminishing numbers we shall not go into a discussion of neighborhood differences on these statistics. It became fairly obvious in the course of examining them, however, that at each step from police contacts to seriousness of contacts to referrals, the inner city and interstitial areas differed more and more from other areas and that there had also been an increasing focus on youthful offenders.

Cohort, Age, Time Period, and Spatial Variation in Court Sanctions

Assuming that the apparent focus of attention on youthful offenders continues one step further, we would expect even more distinct differences between inner city and interstitial areas and other areas in the community when severity of sanctions scores are considered. We should note that there was a sharp jump in the percent of those who had been sanctioned between the 1949 and 1955 Cohorts as well as an increase in the average severity of sanctions scores for these cohorts.

The consequences of this are problematic in reference to our maje hypothesis that delinquency and crime areas move outward from the inne city with population movement and with change in the organization c society. It does appear that concern with youthful offenders resulted i comparatively more of them being sanctioned from some areas from th 1955 Cohort than would be expected considering the comparative positio of these areas on frequency of contacts and seriousness of reasons fc contact.

We concluded: (1) that age group/cohort sanctions patterns did nc coincide perfectly with other contact, seriousness, and referral patterns fo the inner city and interstitial areas when, in fact, they should be a logice outgrowth of them; (2) that concerns about the problems of juveni delinquency and youthful crime have led to the application of more sever sanctions to juveniles in the late teen-age group in the most recent tim period (an age group emphasis on severity of sanctions as a deterrent te future criminality); (3) that this has resulted in the disproportiona involvement of juveniles with the justice system from some areas outsid the inner city and interstitial areas; (4) that deviations from the transitio model for other measures of delinquency and crime may be fostered b changes in the social organization of the city as manifested in the changin; characteristics of areas; and (5) that the cyclical nature of events in th justice system (the consequences of sanctions on future behavior) ha probably played a part in creating deviations from the inherently spatia nature of the expected pattern of contacts and seriousness of offenses from cohort to cohort and age group to age group.

The Hardening of the Inner City

It was apparent that public concern about juvenile delinquency anc youthful crime had led to the application of more severe sanctions in the most recent time period and that this had led to disproportional justice system involvement of juveniles in some areas outside the inner city anc transitional areas. Change in population composition as a consequence o movement (Skogman, 1979; Greenwood, Petersilia, and Zimring, 1980), particularly if it involved the movement of Non-Whites into sectors of the city which had traditionally been White, focused attention on an area and, in all probability, increased its police contact and referral rates. Public perception of the nature of an area, even though incorrect, may lead to the area becoming the way that they believe it to be. The cyclical nature o events in the justice system (the consequences of sanctions on future behavior) has probably played a part in creating more recent deviations from the expected pattern of contacts and seriousness of offenses from cohort to cohort and time period to time period (Ageton and Elliott, 1974).

Further examination of patterns of change led us to refer to the general pattern of spatial relationships between delinquency and crime and the social and ecological structure of the city as "the hardening of the inner city" (Shannon, 1986a). Although not a new point (Murphy, 1977; Platt, 1969; Leopold, 1958; Krisberg and Austin, 1978; Empey, 1982), we see the hardening of the inner city as a factor in the development of the ecological patterns of delinquency and crime which have lent support to theories of their generation and perpetuation. These data do not, of course, provide support for race/ethnic explanations of delinquency and crime (Blau and Blau, 1982; Watts and Watts, 1981).

What was demonstrated most specifically by multivariate analyses of the neighborhood data was that neighborhood SES as represented by housing quality (housing quality itself was not considered to be a "cause") had remained an important influence on delinquency and crime rates in the 1970s. Compared to the impact of the ecological variables, however, offense rates during the 1960s had more powerful effects on rates in the 1970s. That is, the Adjusted R^2 increased from .852 to .925 when ecological variables were added to the 1960 offense rates, a relatively small increase. Conversely, ecological variables accounted for less than 23% of the variance in 1970 neighborhood offense rates but R^2 increased from .227 to .925 when 1960 offense rates were added.

In terms of the support that ecological analyses lent to structural theory, we believed that additional research with neighborhoods might enable us to account for even more of the variation in police contacts, offense rates, referrals, and severity of sanctions that appeared to be developing and which had given rise to our concept, "the hardening of the inner city."

Note

1. The second major project in the series, *The Relationship of Juvenile Delinquency and Adult Crime to the Changing Ecological Structure of the City* (Shannon, 1982), was funded by the National Institute of Justice, Grant Number 79-NI-AX-0081.

Chapter 4

THE DEVELOPMENT OF SERIOUS CRIMINAL CAREERS AND THE DELINQUENT NEIGHBORHOOD

The Neighborhood in Theory and Research

People in the community perceive some neighborhoods as breeding grounds for delinquency and crime. Researchers may have general concurrence with community perceptions, differing to a degree because they have data on who commits what types of offenses where and the incidence of serious offenses in various neighborhoods over lengthy periods of time. They are also aware of the fact that many people in the inner city are kinder and gentler than their neighbors in the suburbs. Nevertheless, we must take cognizance of the fact that many people do think of delinquent neighborhoods and places where the incidence of visible crime is high as the dangerous areas in which most delinquent and criminal types live or congregate.

Research reveals that the picture is exceedingly complex; some neighborhoods are highly productive of delinquents and criminals, others contain institutions or establishments that are arenas for delinquency and crime, and still others contain both the social conditions and the institutions that produce high in-area and by place of residence rates of delinquency and crime. Sociologists go beyond this when they hypothesize that community perceptions of people in some neighborhoods ultimately generate different official responses to their delinquent and criminal behavior, tending to produce the continuities in delinquent and criminal careers that intensify the delinquency and crime in these neighborhoods. As a consequence, officially recorded rates of delinquency and crime become even higher than they would otherwise be, if only as the product of social interaction in these neighborhoods.

The relatively consistent relationships which we have found between neighborhood characteristics and delinquency and crime rates lends support, as we have said, to more than one sociological explanation. These neighborhood differences, for example, represent social class or sub-cultural differences and produce milieu effects, i.e., the effects of growing up in a different subculture, the cultural deviation theory.

That some of the most visible conflict also appears between youth from the same social class does not obviate a class conflict argument if gang warfare among lower class youth is seen as a product of a society organized along class lines (Schultz, 1962; Kobrin, Puntil and Peluso, 1967; Ball-Rokeach, 1973; Thornberry and Sagarin, 1972; Erlanger, 1979). At the same time, neighborhoods provide the setting for variation that lends support for differential association, social control, strain, or containment theory, all of which are subsumed under social process theory.

Even if emphasis was placed on referral rates, severity of sanctions, and disproportional (to offense seriousness) severity of sanctions, it would still be difficult to reject any group of theories because it could well be said that each plays a part in accounting for the totality of variation in delinquency and crime. This is, of course, why there has been a call for integrative theories.

An integrated theory may combine elements of social structure, social process, social conflict, and other more or less general theories in a way that accounts for much of the delinquency in a cohort but still may not be useful to persons on the firing line who are concerned about prevention and/or resocialization of delinquents. Some sociological explanations account for differences in delinquency and crime between neighborhoods and some account for differences in the seriousness of delinquent and/or criminal careers among those who live within the same types of neighborhoods. While all of this may seem repetitious, our point is that a variety of explanations or combinations of explanations based on variables which are encapsulated by neighborhoods or indicative of types of life experiences may still be much more useful in accounting for differences in delinquency and crime rates than are explanations which are based on kinds of people.

Classifying Neighborhoods as
Delinquency and Crime Producing

Delinquency and crime producing characteristics are those aspects of the neighborhood milieu which are hypothesized to make it an arena for learning patterns of delinquent and criminal behavior and rationalizations for these behaviors. Sociologists have traditionally used measures of land use, housing quality, occupational level, marital status, and other demographic indices as indicators of neighborhood milieu. In addition, where available they have utilized such attitudinal data as would suggest that the population of the neighborhood has not been integrated into the larger society, has absorbed or internalized a lower class subculture, or has attitudes receptive to deviant behavior.

The incidence and prevalence of crime have, of course, been primary indicators that a neighborhood is delinquency and crime producing, a not entirely circular type of reasoning because each generation becomes a role model for those which follow. How people in the community perceive their own and other neighborhoods, how the media perceive them, how persons in the justice system from police to judges perceive them, become additional independent variables which, in the course of human interaction, have an effect on how everything that happens in an area is perceived and reacted to. In a real sense, perceptions help create the hardening phenomenon to which we have referred. This is a step beyond the already accepted position that non-legal factors account for some disproportional sanctioning of individual offenders (Blumstein, Cohen, Martin, and Tonry, 1983; Petersilia, 1980; Welch, Spohn, and Gruhl, 1985; Zatz, 1984).

The analysis of how neighborhood differences produce different types and rates of delinquency and crime and continuity of careers within and between delinquent and criminal careers that follow is presented in some detail. Each of the sixty-five neighborhoods was categorized according to its Delinquency and Crime Producing Characteristics (DCPs), In-Area Offense Rates, By-Residence Offense Rates, Juvenile Delinquency Rates, and Adult Crime Rates.[1]

A number of different approaches to categorizing neighborhoods by juvenile and adult in-area and by place of residence offense rates were tried, some in which the data were utilized in a judgmental fashion and some in which the data were computer-manipulated to create clusters with programs such as SAS FASTCLUS.[2] This enabled us to determine the extent to which various independent assessments of what neighborhoods were like (characteristics hypothesized to be productive of delinquency and crime or continuing delinquency and crime) were related to a variety of cohort measures of delinquency and crime. It presented a more precise test of the theories which hypothesized that the variables which generate delinquency may be spatially delineated, although not necessarily in concentric zones (Park, Burgess, and McKenzie, 1925) or sectors (Hoyt, 1939).

The distribution of forty-nine neighborhoods which had sufficient cohort members for the various statistical analyses is shown in Map 4.1 as they occur within the city and as exploded according to Inner City, Transitional, Stable, and Peripheral. Most neighborhoods with

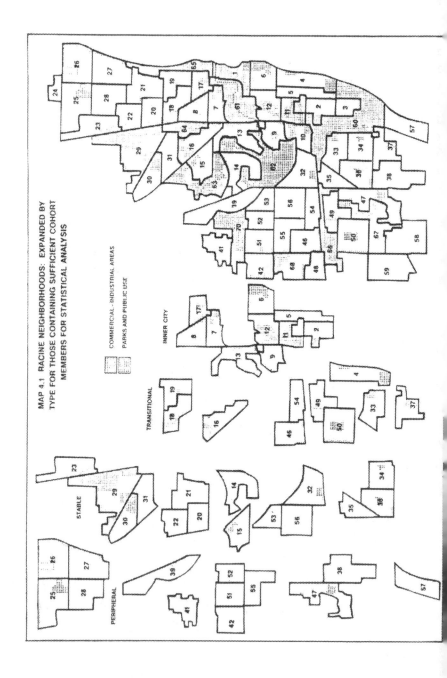

MAP 4.1 RACINE NEIGHBORHOODS: EXPANDED BY
TYPE FOR THOSE CONTAINING SUFFICIENT COHORT
MEMBERS FOR STATISTICAL ANALYSIS

consistently high measures of delinquency and crime are in the inner city and those with low rates are most likely to be peripheral neighborhoods.

No matter how the neighborhoods were ranked as delinquency and crime producing or as having high offense rates in a total of nineteen ranking systems, there were fourteen neighborhoods which almost invariably had the highest possible score. All save three were in the inner city and these three were in transitional areas. There were also eleven neighborhoods with the lowest scores on almost every one of the nineteen ranking systems and all except one were in the middle to upper SES or outlying neighborhoods. The consistency in neighborhood ranks that we found indicates that the association of DCPs and offense rates are not an artifact of any single ranking system. Some of the most distinguishing differences between neighborhoods are shown in Table 4.1. The percent of a neighborhood's residents who were Black is presented only to indicate the kinds of neighborhoods in which Blacks were socialized, the kinds of neighborhoods in which they grew up, and, for that matter, in which most reside throughout their lives.

Disproportional Involvement in the Justice System

Our working hypothesis at this stage of the research was that at each stage of the judicial process from police contacts to sanctions, cohort members from neighborhoods with high DCPs and high rates from other measurement series would have disproportionately higher scores on any measure of involvement in delinquency and crime. These cohort members would have disproportionately higher scores from contacts to severity of sanctions because the justice system operates differently depending on how judges perceive neighborhoods as having or not having a threatening situation with which they should deal. The analyses were carried out with a variety of strategies but little support for this extreme position was found. Variation in neighborhood characteristics did not tend to have a *greater* and *greater* relationship to measures of justice system involvement as offenders progressed from police contacts to court sanctions.

For example, the distribution of 117 delinquency and crime experience types based on frequency of contact, seriousness of offenses, frequency of referral, and severity of sanctions (represented by Geometric scores)[3] indicating the progressive involvement of cohort members in the justice system revealed that a wide variety of juvenile and adult experience types were found in each cohort and in *each* category or cluster of neighborhoods. While the cumulative nature of careers revealed that intervention was more often followed by continuity than discontinuity, the correlation between juvenile and adult types was only modest (ranked

TABLE 4.1 NEIGHBORHOOD OFFENSE, DCP, AND DEMOGRAPHIC CHARACTERISTICS: OFFENSE SERIOUSNESS, REFERRAL, AND SANCTION QUARTILES OF COMBINED COHORTS

| | Offense Rates | | | | | | | | | | | Quartiles | | | | | |
| | INAREA | | BYRES | | JUVENILE | | ADULT | | DCP | | %BLACK | JUV | | | ADULT | | |
NBHD	CMP (1)	CUS (2)	CMP (3)	CUS (4)	CMP (5)	CUS (6)	CMP (7)	CUS (8)	CMP (9)	CUS (10)		OFFREFERD	SER	SANCT	OFFREFERD	SER	SANCT
Inner City Neighborhoods																	
2	H	H	H	H	H	M	H	H	H	H	70	1	2	3	1	1	1
7	H	H	H	H	H	H	H	H	H	H	45	1	1	1	1	1	1
8	H	H	H	H	H	M	H	H	H	H	37	1	1	1	1	2	1
9	H	H	H	H	H	M	H	H	H	H	80	1	1	2	1	1	1
11	H	H	H	H	L	H	H	H	H	H	50	1	1	1	1	1	1
12	H	H	H	H	H	H	H	H	H	H	46	1	1	1	1	1	1
13	H	H	H	H	H	M	H	H	H	M	35	1	1	1	1	1	1
10	H	H	H	M	H	H	H	H	H	H	21	2	1	1	2	2	3
17	H	H	H	M	H	M	H	H	H	M	10	1	2	1	1	1	1
5	M	M	H	M	H	M	H	H	H	M	16	3	3	2	3	3	3
6	H	H	H	H	H	H	H	H	M	M	8	1	1	1	1	1	1
Transitional Neighborhoods																	
18	H	H	H	M	H	H	H	H	H	M	2	2	2	2	1	1	2
16	H	M	M	M	L	M	H	H	H	M	17	1	2	4	2	3	2
19	M	M	H	M	H	M	H	M	H	M	0	2	2	2	2	2	2
49	H	M	H	M	H	M	H	H	M	M	6	2	1	1	2	1	1
46	M	M	H	M	H	M	H	H	M	M	3	1	1	2	1	1	1
54	M	L	H	L	L	M	L	M	M	M	1	2	1	3	2	2	2
50	M	M	M	M	L	M	H	M	L	L	1	2	3	1	2	1	2
4	M	M	L	L	L	L	H	H	M	M	2	4	4	4	4	4	4
33	M	M	M	L	H	L	H	M	M	M	4	3	3	3	4	2	2
37	L	L	H	M	L	M	L	M	M	M	10	1	1	2	1	1	1
Stable Residential Neighborhoods																	
14	M	M	L	L	H	L	L	M	M	M	0	2	2	4	3	2	2
15	L	L	M	L	L	M	L	M	M	M	0	1	3	3	2	3	2
20	M	M	M	L	H	L	L	M	M	M	0	4	3	3	4	3	4
21	L	L	L	L	L	L	L	M	M	L	0	4	4	3	3	4	4
22	L	L	L	L	L	L	L	M	M	M	0	4	4	4	3	4	4
23	H	M	M	L	H	M	H	H	M	M	2	2	2	2	4	3	3
29	M	M	M	M	L	M	H	H	M	L	0	2	4	4	2	2	3
30	H	H	M	M	H	H	L	H	L	L	0	2	1	1	3	4	4
31	L	L	M	L	L	M	L	M	L	L	0	2	2	3	2	2	2
32	M	M	L	L	L	L	L	M	M	M	1	3	4	4	3	4	4
34	M	M	M	M	H	M	L	L	L	L	0	3	2	1	3	4	2
35	M	M	M	L	L	L	L	M	M	M	0	4	3	3	4	3	4
36	L	L	M	L	L	L	L	M	L	M	0	3	2	3	4	3	3
53	L	L	L	L	L	L	L	M	M	M	0	4	3	4	3	3	3
56	M	M	M	M	H	M	L	M	M	M	0	3	3	2	2	2	2
Peripheral Middle to High SES Neighborhoods																	
25	M	M	M	M	L	L	H	L	L	L	0	4	4	4	4	4	4
26	M	L	L	L	L	L	L	L	L	L	0	4	3	3	4	4	3
27	L	L	L	L	L	L	L	L	L	L	0	4	4	3	3	3	3
28	L	L	M	L	L	L	L	L	L	L	0	4	4	2	4	4	4
39	L	L	L	L	L	L	L	L	L	L	0	4	3	4	4	4	3
41	L	L	M	L	H	L	H	L	L	L	0	3	2	2	4	4	4
42	M	M	L	L	L	L	L	L	L	L	0	3	3	3	4	3	3
51	L	L	L	L	L	L	L	M	L	L	0	3	4	2	3	4	3
52	L	L	L	L	L	L	L	L	L	L	0	4	4	4	4	4	4
55	L	L	M	L	L	L	H	M	M	L	1	3	4	4	2	4	2
47	M	M	H	L	H	L	H	H	L	L	0	3	2	1	2	2	3
38	L	L	M	L	H	M	L	M	L	L	0	2	4	4	3	2	2
57	L	L	L	L	L	L	L	M	L	M	0	4	4	4	4	3	4

Geometric scores for juveniles and adults correlated .578 for the 1942 Cohort, .596 for the 1949 Cohort, and .524 for the 1955 Cohort).

When misbehavior and involvement with the justice system were related to characteristics of the home neighborhood, the evidence that milieu accounted for a progressive (over time) relationship of careers to neighborhood characteristics was not strong unless the focus was on inner city vs. all other neighborhoods. Here the evidence was much clearer but still not definitive. For example, five different Geometric scores (out of the 117 possibilities) that culminated in high sanctions during the juvenile period contained 3.3% of all scores for the 1955 Cohort but contained *8.0% of the scores for those who resided in neighborhoods high in DCP characteristics or high by-residence offense rate neighborhoods.* When considering the ten different Geometric types culminating in high sanctions, we find that 52.3% of all cohort members with one of these highly sanctioned types of juvenile careers were from inner city neighborhoods, although only 24.4% of the combined cohorts resided there as juveniles.

The corresponding figures for adults were 46.8% of the highly sanctioned types vs. 20.2% of the cohort members who resided in the inner city as adults. The decline from the inner city to the peripheral neighborhoods for juveniles with these types of careers, in percentages, was 52.3, 23.0, 15.3, and 9.2. The percentages for adults were equally striking, 46.8, 24.3, 18.0, and 10.8. The 9.2% and 10.8% of the cohorts who resided in peripheral neighborhoods and who were in highly sanctioned types constituted less than half of the 22.1% of the juveniles and 22.6% of the adults who resided there.

Whichever way one looks at it neighborhood milieu plays an important part in determining juvenile and adult experiences and perceptions and subsequent delinquent or non-delinquent behavior. When the expected pattern is not found, there are usually variables that, if they had been

1   Table 1, The Development of Serious Criminal Careers and the Delinquent Neighborhood, and Tables 1A, 1B, and 2, Appendix A in above (from The Relationship of Juvenile Delinquency and Adult Crime to the Changing Ecological Structure of the City, Chapter 7, Table 2).
2   Table 3 and Appendix C, Tables 9 and 10, The Development, clusters 4 and 3 - High, 2 - Medium, and 1 - Low.
3   Table 1 and Appendix A, The Development, Chapter 7, Table 7, The Relationship.
4   Table 4 and Appendix C, Tables 5 and 6, The Development, clusters 6 and 5 - High, 4 and 3 - Medium, and 2 and 1 - Low.
5   Table 2 and Appendix A, Table 2, The Development.
6   Table 5 and Appendix A, Table 13, The Development.
7   Table 2 and Appendix A, Table 3, The Development.
8   Table 6 and Appendix A, Table 17, The Development, clusters 4 and 3 - High, 2 - Medium, and 1 - Low.
9   Table 1 and Appendix A, The Development.
10 Table 3 and Appendix C, Tables 1 and 2, The Development, cluster 6 - High, cluster 4 - Medium, and Clusters 3, 2, and 1 - Low.
11 Table 25, The Development.

considered differently, might have produced more order than that which was observed. Neighborhood 5, for example, is directly behind the Old Gold Coast (Neighborhood 4) but its transition to the inner city was almost complete. At the same time, it was not following the normal pattern of transition because the University of Wisconsin-Parkside, later to become Gateway Technical, was located in this area. Neighborhood 5 might better have been placed in transition and Neighborhood 4 left in the stable residential group. Neighborhood 18, although grouped with transitionals, might better have been considered part of the inner city. Be all that as it may, there is still an element of regularity between neighborhood groupings, DCPs, composite and cluster classifications, and the offense seriousness, referral, and sanctions rates.

A Further Look at Consistency in Measures and Continuity in Careers

In Table 4.2 neighborhoods were clustered according to the delinquent and criminal behavior of cohort residents and court reactions to their behavior (consistency) and according to the relationship of cohort members' juvenile to adult records (continuity). The variables were: (1) consistency (interrelatedness of number of contacts, seriousness of offense, frequency of referral, and severity of sanctions) in either the juvenile or adult period and (2) continuity in careers from juvenile to adult. Consistency *and* continuity were more complex phenomena than continuity alone as dealt with in Blumstein, Cohen, Roth, and Visher (1986).

Consistency in juvenile measures was relatively high in high DCP, inner city neighborhoods that had high by-residence offense rates. There were, however, some neighborhoods outside the inner city whose residents had similar juvenile consistency involving high scores on all measures. Although there were neighborhoods whose residents had consistency in measurements during one period but not during the other, most of the inner city neighborhoods were characterized by consistency during both periods.

The juvenile and adult periods were more closely linked (continuity) in high DCP inner city and transitional neighborhoods which also had high in-area offense rates or by-residence rates. The phenomenon of sanctions during the juvenile period followed by sanctions during the adult period was more characteristic of inner city neighborhoods than other neighborhoods. However, only modest support appeared for the hypothesis that differences in neighborhood milieus (as they had been defined and classified into four types, i.e., inner city, transitional, etc.), produced variation not only in delinquent and criminal behavior but in

TABLE 4.2 CONSISTENCY, CONTINUITY, OFFENSE SERIOUSNESS, SEVERITY OF SANCTIONS, AND DISPROPORTIONAL INTERVENTION AND SANCTIONING

NGHBD	CONSIST JUV	CONSIST ADULT	CONTINUITY [1]	DISPRO SANCT J [2]	DISPRO SANCT A	M SERIOUSNESS J	M SERIOUSNESS A	M SS SEV SS SANCTS J	M SS SEV SS SANCTS A	DISPRO INTER J [3]	DISPRO INTER A	SEVER SANCTS F [4]	SEVER SANCTS M
Inner City Neighborhoods													
2	J			123	63	H	H			.311	.488	20.5	14.5
7	J	A		51	123	H	H	H	H	.462	.595	34.8	21.9
8	J	A		63	35	H	H	H	H	.353	.488	26.3	18.0
9	J	A	C	59	123	H	H	H	H	.324	.533	22.5	8.0
11	J	A	C	43	57	H	H	H	H	.400	.588	37.2	19.2
12	J	A	C	120	42	H	H	H	H	.739	.520	26.8	12.6
13	J	A	C	59	61	H	H	H	H	.457	.548	15.4	14.8
10		A		95	53	H	H		H	.350	.500	28.6	11.9
17	J	A		43	123	H	H	H	H	.240	.400	27.4	14.6
5	J	A		30	20					.217	.200	36.1	12.4
6	J	A	C	62	23			H	H	.583	.500	43.6	9.2
Transitional Neighborhoods													
18	J	A	C	42	62	H	H	H	H	.238	.421	32.3	15.0
16				30	9		H			.214	.240	19.6	10.2
19	J	A	C	50	43	H	H	H	H	.348	.280	21.3	13.7
49	J	A	C	49	61	H	H	H	H	.944	.000	40.9	8.4
46	J	A	C	63	62	H	H		H	.281	.290	31.1	16.3
54	J		C	127	95	H	H		H	.346	.286	15.8	7.4
50	J	A	C	27	10	H				.154	.148	23.3	9.2
4				2	4					.071	.000	----	4.9
33	J	A	C	13	21					.200	.500	----	8.5
37	J	A		43	50	H	H	H	H	.238	.857	36.7	21.5
Stable Residential Neighborhoods													
14		A		19	28					.250	.240	----	8.0
15				55	46			H	H	.269	.174	----	5.7
20	J			32	39					.500	.222	----	12.2
21	J			13	22					.100	.235	----	11.9
22	J			4	35					.167	.188	----	14.4
23	J			18	20					.261	.462	21.6	15.4
29		A	C	6	110					.059	.333	18.3	12.1
30	J		C	29	2					.273	.100	----	10.2
31	J	A		14	35					.154	.257	----	7.6
32				23	18					.158	.323	20.5	10.8
34	J	A		28	3					.400	.118	48.0	18.8
35	J			14	84					.105	.357	26.0	12.4
36	J	A	C	17	20					.393	.333	----	13.2
53	J	A	C	4	9					.250	.200	----	10.0
56	J	A		2	30					.167	.231	26.8	8.0
Peripheral Middle to High SES Neighborhoods													
25	J	A		2	5					.105	.200	37.4	16.8
26		A		20	0					.500	.250	----	3.8
27				4	68					.100	.250	----	12.0
28	J	A		65	12					.238	.048	7.8	5.6
39	J	A		4	17					.300	.167	----	8.3
41		A		85	1					.429	.143	----	9.8
42	J			28	17					.143	.400	----	6.0
51	J	A	C	66	2					.154	.083	----	----
52	J			4	21					.182	.300	----	8.0
55				21	66					.111	.130	----	11.6
47	J	A	C	41	33					.333	.474	12.0	11.3
38		A		39	28					.148	.389	28.7	8.4
57	J	A		84	16					.267	.545	----	10.5

1 Table 19, The Development of Serious Criminal Careers and the Delinquent Neighborhood.
2 Table 28, The Development.
3 Table 29, The Development.
4 Table 31, The Development.

even *more* pronounced (disproportional) societal reactions (police and court experiences) as represented by the next two columns of figures in Table 4.2.

In sum, the elaborate steps taken to represent the consistency of relationships between variables during the juvenile and adult periods and continuity between periods culminated in a series of tables, as encapsulated in the first five columns of Table 4.2, which provided little evidence of systematic change in relationships from one end of the continuum of neighborhoods to the other. They did suggest, however that high offense rate and high DCP neighborhoods were more likely to have cohort members with high seriousness, referral, and sanctions scores, more consistency in the relationship of seriousness, referrals, and sanctions for cohort members during both age periods, and more continuity in careers between age periods than was found in other types of neighborhoods.

Furthermore, those twenty-three neighborhoods with consistency absent in either the juvenile or the adult period were, with two exceptions, outside the inner city and interstitial neighborhoods. All but two of the inner city neighborhoods presented a fairly consistent relationship between the level of delinquent and criminal behavior and the level of involvement of their cohort members with the justice system (columns 6-9, Table 4.2).

Although the significant concentration of high seriousness and high intervention types in the inner city and transitional neighborhoods was not followed by the same concentration in disproportional intervention scores (columns 10-13, Table 4.2), neighborhood milieu did account for almost 40% of the variance in intervention scores.[4] The consequences of being "bad" were recognizable in the inner city areas and in some other neighborhoods as well. Just why there was disproportional intervention in these neighborhoods we do not know. We also found that being socialized in a high offense rate and high DCP neighborhood had more formative effects on total careers even if subsequent movement was to a "better" neighborhood than did the formative effects good neighborhoods had on those with downward movement to neighborhoods with less desirable milieus.

It might appear that experimenting with a variety of measures and procedures was a departure from rigorous research methodology in which hypotheses are tested and accepted or rejected, but this is the way that it sometimes works out in the real world of research. The aim was to determine if reorganization of the data in different ways would produce an interrelationship of variables accounting for a sufficient amount of the variance to permit accurate prediction of the dependent variables (juvenile and adult behavior and justice system experience) from the independent variables (neighborhood milieu).

In the end, we concluded that significant milieu effects as represented by a broad range of DCPs and in-area and by-residence offense rates were related to cohort offense, referral, and sanctions rates but accounted for only small amounts of the variance in consistency and continuity in individual official careers. Even though measures of the seriousness of officially recorded delinquent and criminal careers, self-reported seriousness, and disproportional intervention were higher in inner city and interstitial neighborhoods than in others, consistency and continuity had less relationship to neighborhood milieu differences. Consistency and continuity were also present in neighborhoods with quite different characteristics from those of the inner city.

What Goes on Inside Each Neighborhood?

The next step was an analysis of individuals within the neighborhood which utilized the relationship (Pearsonian coefficients) of each cohort member's score on one measure to that same member's score on another measure. Although most of the analyses referred to in this chapter have been based on the behavior of cohort members by place of juvenile socialization, in the analyses to which we now refer the adult correlations were based on place of juvenile residence and then adult residence.

The juvenile period correlations between offense seriousness and severity of sanctions, without regard to neighborhood, were .598 for the 1949 Cohort and .735 for the 1955 Cohort. The adult period correlations based on juvenile residence were .565 and .717 but when shifted to adult residence were .584 and .730, indicating, as we said before, that juvenile residence (place of socialization) was a major determinant of adult behavior. There were, of course, some neighborhoods in which the correlations between offense seriousness and adult sanctions dropped when adult place of residence determined which cohort members were included in the correlation. These were scattered throughout the city rather than showing any pattern of concentration.

Most of the 135 within-neighborhood correlations (1949 and 1955 Cohorts for thirty-four neighborhoods with sufficient cohort members) between *offense seriousness and severity of sanctions* were sizable (table not included but eighty-two of the 135 coefficients of correlation were above .700). The ten inner city neighborhoods produced positive relationships between offense seriousness and severity of sanctions with only one exception, the only neighborhood with less than 10% Black population. These inner city neighborhoods had high in-area and

by-residence offense rates, high juvenile and adult offense rates, hig
DCP characteristics, and, except for three, 35% or more Black residen*
as of 1970. We have usually taken the position that the cohorts are n*
samples and have not been too concerned about statistical significance, b*
it should be noted that even with the small Ns of neighborhoods, most *
these relationships were significant at least at the .05 level.

The picture was similar for transitional neighborhoods, although ther
were several in which the relationship between juvenile *offense seriousnes*
and severity of sanctions differed markedly from that for the adult perioc
This was most noticeable in Neighborhood 16 (.365 for the juvenile perio
vs. .908 for the adult period), which also had the highest percent Black.
Although there was considerably less juvenile/adult consistency when th*
stable residential and peripheral middle to high SES neighborhoods wer
considered, over half showed sizable relationships between offens*
seriousness and severity of sanctions.

The Inner City vs. Other Neighborhoods

In order to make the difference between inner city and the othe*
neighborhoods clearer, the dichotomized distribution of offens*
seriousness and severity of sanctions for 1942 and 1949 Cohort member
referred at the time of police contact are shown in Table 4.3. The grea*
majority of every group appears in the category of "below the mean o*
career seriousness" (and had also received less severe sanctions) because
as we have so frequently said, a small percent of each group accounted fo*
a large percent of the offenses of that group and even a larger percent o*
the serious offenses (thus the mean is far above the mid-point).

In every group the proportion of inner city serious offenders (above th*
mean) who received severe sanctions (above the mean) was greater for th*
1955 Cohort than for the 1949 Cohort. Had the 1942 Cohort been show*
in those groups for which there were sufficient persons, it would have ha*
the lowest proportion of serious offenders who were severely sanctioned.

Increases in the proportion of serious offenders who were severely
sanctioned were greater for Non-Whites than Whites, as were increase*
for Whites in the inner city greater than they were for Whites from othe*
neighborhoods. The most pronounced change in severity of sanctions fo*
juveniles above the mean in seriousness was for Non-Whites from inne*
city neighborhoods. In the two White groups, inner city and othe*
neighborhoods, the proportion of less serious offenders who were severely
sanctioned increased more than did the proportion of similar Non-White
inner city persons. Less serious offenders who were Non-White had abou*
the same proportion of less serious offenders severely sanctioned as di*

TABLE 4.3   RELATIONSHIP OF JUVENILE OFFENSE SERIOUSNESS TO
SEVERITY OF SANCTIONS BY NEIGHBORHOOD TYPE AND RACE
FOR PERSONS REFERRED: 1949 AND 1955 COHORTS

INNER CITY NEIGHBORHOODS

		1949				1955		
				Non-White				
		Severity of Sanctions				Severity of Sanctions		
		Mean-	Mean+			Mean-	Mean+	
Offense Seriousness	M+	19.4	5.6	25.0	M+	1.9	17.9	19.8
	M-	66.7	8.3	75.0	M-	70.8	9.4	80.2
		86.1	13.9	100.0%		72.7	27.3	100.0%
		Pearson's R = .187 ns				Pearson's R = .731		

		White						
		Severity of Sanctions				Severity of Sanctions		
		Mean-	Mean+			Mean-	Mean+	
Offense Seriousness	M+	11.1	11.1	22.2	M+	5.7	17.1	22.8
	M-	75.9	1.9	77.8	M-	68.6	8.6	77.2
		87.0	13.0	100.0%		74.3	25.7	100.0%
		Pearson's R = .630				Pearson's R = .674		

OTHER NEIGHBORHOODS

		White						
		Severity of Sanctions				Severity of Sanctions		
		Mean-	Mean+			Mean-	Mean+	
Offense Seriousness	M+	3.6	4.1	7.7	M+	2.6	6.8	9.4
	M-	88.8	3.6	92.4	M-	82.6	7.9	90.5
		92.4	7.7	100.1%		85.2	14.7	99.9%
		Pearson's R = .551				Pearson's R = .564		

	1949	1955
Mean Cohort Juvenile Seriousness	17.5	22.6
Non-White Inner City	24.7	31.6
White Inner City	24.8	25.5
White Other Neighborhoods	13.3	17.1
Mean Cohort Severity of Sanctions	2.2	6.7
Non-White Inner City	3.5	8.0
White Inner City	2.2	8.1
White Other Neighborhoods	1.6	5.8

the inner city Whites. The inner city Non-Whites had the highe
Pearson's R (.731) for the undichotomized data. Inner city Whites a
Non-Whites had a larger proportion of their less serious offens
sanctioned than did Whites who resided outside the inner city.

These patterned juvenile relationships showed less cohort change f
adults (1942 vs. 1949 Cohort comparisons were more appropriate becau:
of the limited adult exposure of the 1955 Cohort). Here again, serior
Non-White offenders from the inner city (1949 Cohort) had the large
proportion of their relatively serious offenders severely sanctioned. It w:
also apparent that relatively more of the serious Non-White offenders fro
other neighborhoods as well as the inner city received more seve
sanctions as compared with White groups for the 1949 Cohort, but th
difference had been markedly reduced for the 1955 Cohort.

The relationship of offense seriousness to the disproportionality c
sanctions index also received further consideration. The results showe
that leniency for those above the mean in seriousness had declined mor
sharply for inner city Non-Whites than Whites, although both had decline
significantly. At the same time, the proportion of less serious offende
who were dealt with leniently remained about the same for both White
and Non-Whites and increased for Whites in other neighborhoods.

The decline in leniency for serious adult offenders was most apparer
for inner city Non-Whites, but was accompanied by an increase i
leniency for less serious offenders. Changes in court severity i
relationship to the seriousness of offenses were more apparent in thei
effects on the careers of juveniles than adults.

Summary

What has all of this told us beyond some additional affirmation of th
position that delinquency and crime and delinquent and criminal career:
are produced at higher rates in areas expected to be productive of then
than in areas which have traditionally not provided the climate an
rationalizations for ordinary delinquency and crime? We can say that th
cumulative severity of sanctions is related to cumulative offens
seriousness, more in the inner city than in other neighborhoods, mos
consistently during the juvenile period for the 1955 Cohort. When w
turn to disproportional sanctioning, there is less consistency betwee
offense seriousness and disproportional sanctioning outside the inner city

It is difficult. however, to encapsulate the data so as to say witl
assurance that those who resided in neighborhoods which had high offens
rates and were conceptualized as being delinquency and crime producing
were perceived by persons in the justice system as residing in a

neighborhood milieu whose residents should receive consideration for their offenses different from those who resided in other neighborhoods. In sum, however, the data do suggest that serious offenders from inner city neighborhoods are dealt with severely while those who reside outside the inner city may or may not be dealt with as rigorously. Most of all, it is apparent that those who resided in the inner city, particularly Blacks from the 1955 Cohort, were not dealt with more leniently than had been those who preceded them from older cohorts.

Notes

1. The third major project in the series, *The Development of Serious Criminal Careers and the Delinquent Neighborhood* (Shannon, 1984), was funded by the National Institute of Juvenile Justice and Delinquency Prevention, Grant Number 82-JN-AX-0004.

2. The average population of neighborhoods was 1,424 in 1950, 1,524 in 1960, and 1,555 in 1970, but dropped to 1,343 in 1980 with the addition of peripheral neighborhoods and the decline of the inner city population.

Our larger report to NIJJDP (Shannon, 1984) contains several lengthy chapters and statistical appendixes describing how block data from the 1960, 1970, and 1980 Censuses were utilized in developing DCPs for neighborhoods. Ten variables, including housing quality, density, vacancy, population characteristics, population trends, land use, and target density, were utilized in the computer clustering procedures. This built on the ecological research reported in *The Relationship of Juvenile Delinquency and Adult Crime to the Changing Ecological Structure of the City, op. cit.* These chapters and appendixes also show how different types of offense rates were combined to produce neighborhood in-area offense rates (five variables used), by-residence offense rates (six variables used), and so on. As far as measures of the seriousness of individual careers is concerned, these were first developed for and reported in *Assessing the Relationship of Adult Criminal Careers to Juvenile Careers, op. cit.*

There were originally twenty-six categories of police contacts which were reduced to felonies against persons, felonies against property, major misdemeanors, minor misdemeanors, status offenses, and contacts for suspicion, investigation, or information in the development of a simple additive seriousness scale, 6 for felonies against persons to 1 for contact for suspicion, investigation, or information. This is admittedly a legalistic approach to seriousness but it does lie behind the severity of sanctions that may be meted out by the courts. There were originall eight categories of police referral but these were dichotomized becaus most fell into "counselled and released" or, if referred, to the Count Probation Department or District Attorney. The severity of sanction scale that was ultimately used was ordinal and ranged from dismissed t juvenile institutionalization or confinement in prison.

3.   Among the various measures was a Geometric scale constructed t include data from police contacts to sanctions but emphasizing severity o sanctions as the end result of delinquent and criminal behavior. Unlik a Guttman scale there are no error types in a Geometric scale. Th weights of each item in a scale increase from least serious to most seriou (1, 2, 4, 8, etc.) so that each combination of offenses or sanctions has it own score. This technique makes it possible to see differences in an between neighborhoods based on scores representing frequency of polic contacts, offense seriousness, referrals, severity of sanctions, and th interrelationships of these measures.

4.   We would be remiss not to point out that the complainant fo contacts varies from the inner city to peripheral areas and from contac type to contact type in such a fashion as to suggest that police activity i the inner city has an effect on the basic contact data utilized in ou research. While private citizens were most often the complainants fo some offenses, it was apparent that police played a greater role in th inner city than in other types of neighborhoods.

For example, robbery, burglary, theft, liquor offenses, drugs, anc fraud had the police as complainant more often in the inner city than in other types of neighborhoods. Police were less often the complainants on vagrancy and sex offenses in the inner city. In several other cases the inner city and peripheral areas showed agreement on complainant but not in the transitional or stable residential areas. In the latter, private citizens were the complainant and police were only reacting to their calls.

Chapter 5

VARIATION IN THE PROCESS OF
DEVELOPING SERIOUS CRIMINAL CAREERS

Introduction

That a large proportion of the variance in measures of delinquency and crime as well as the interrelationship of measures of delinquency and crime was unaccounted for by neighborhood characteristics (apart from the fact that inner city neighborhoods with a tradition of delinquency and crime continued to have a tradition of delinquency and crime) meant that we had only commenced to produce a model with sufficient complexity. As has been said, there is no simple answer to complex questions about human behavior.

The analyses which we have been describing excluded race/ethnicity, sex, and age at first police contact as independent explanatory variables. Our earlier research and that of others accounts for much of the variance in delinquency and crime rates by including them but, even with controls for SES and/or type of neighborhood, our understanding of delinquency has advanced little beyond that found in the existing literature.

This was the time to turn to a series of multivariate analyses in our effort to understand how delinquency developed and continued at a greater rate in some neighborhoods than in others. The strategy was to see if there were non-ecologically distributed variables which, even if they had limited variation within some neighborhoods, were distributed within other types of neighborhoods so as to account for more delinquency, crime, and disproportionality of intervention (frequency of intervention and severity of sanctions) than had been previously possible. The question is how inner city males, Whites and Non-Whites, become involved in delinquent behavior and become more likely to continue into adult crime than do their counterparts in other neighborhoods. In what respects do they differ from their female counterparts? If more of the disproportionality in sanctions as well as differences in race/ethnicity and sex could be accounted for by this kind of analysis, the analysis would be even more supportive of social process theories.

Accounting for Variance in Offense
Rate and Intervention Scores

Interview variables indicative of respondents' home condition;
educational experiences, work experiences, etc., were manipulated b
multiple regression techniques to ascertain their relationship to measure
of official and self-report seriousness of delinquency and crime and th
extent to which intervention was in proportion to seriousness of offenses
While our list does not constitute a complete list of the variables whic,
have been utilized in social process research, there are a sufficient numbe
that the analyses provide at least a heuristic example of what may b
achieved by this approach. The variables are listed and briefly described
in Table 5.1, as are official and self-report measures of juvenile and adul
misbehavior and relative severity of intervention to offense seriousness
What we found in the inner city is based on two Whites for ever
Non-White, while other neighborhoods were predominantly White.

The variables which measure official career offense seriousness as a
delinquent and criminal, JUVXN and EIGHTPXN, are based on frequency
and seriousness of police contact type. Cohort members with seriou
delinquent and criminal careers in both inner city and other neighborhood
are predominantly male rather than female. Those interviewed were als
asked to complete a form which questioned them about sixteen behavior
ranging from running away from home to drugs to weapons offenses i
each of four age periods which have now been dichotomized to 6 throug
17 and 18 and older. Each set of responses by age for each item wa
weighted according to offense seriousness to generate the seriousness sum
for the age period scores, SRN617 and SRN18P.

RGEOTH17 and RGEOAF17 are summary measures based on officia
police contact seriousness and frequency and severity of sanctions, again
for ages 6 through 17 and 18 and older. They are rank-ordered score
representing the ratio of contact seriousness to subsequent intervention,
ranging from low offense seriousness not perceived to require intervention
to the highest seriousness which received the severest of sanctions. Non-
White males had a mean adult seriousness score of 18.2 while White
males had a score of 15.0 but the mean offense seriousness/intervention
score for Non-Whites was 4.2 while that for Whites was only 2.0. Thus,
the proportional differences between White and Non-White males was far
greater when disproportional severity of intervention was considered than
when it was a matter of official seriousness of offenses alone. These
variables were distributed more or less systematically by Offense Rate
Groups and Delinquency and Crime Producing Groups.

TABLE 5.1 INTERVIEW VARIABLES AND MEASURES OF DELINQUENCY AND CRIME UTILIZED
IN REGRESSION ANALYSES

Transition Measures
AGEDLR   Age Driver License Received
AGEMARRY   Age at Marriage

Home Conditions
INCHH   Sex of Income-Producing Head of Household
HHEMP   Head of Household Regularly Employed

Employment
FIRSTJOB   First Job Level
JOBHSR   Employed During High School

Education
ATTSCHR   Attitude Toward School
NODIPLOMR   Dropout Before High School Graduation

World View
ATTPOLR   Attitude Toward Police
PATROLR   Perceived Police Patrolling in Neighborhood
SELF617   Delinquent Self-Evaluation as Juvenile

Associations
ADJFRTR   Juvenile Friends in Trouble
ADAUTOSC   Auto Use as Juvenile
MILITR   Military Service

Current Status
MARITAL   Marital Status
AFRDSCAL   Adult Friends in Trouble

Juvenile Delinquency (6-17)
JUVXN   Seriousness of Juvenile Police Contacts
SRN617   Self-Report Seriousness of Juvenile Behavior
RGEOTH17   Juvenile Offense Seriousness/Intervention

Adult Crime (18+)
EIGHTPXN   Seriousness of Adult Police Contacts
SRN18P   Self-Report Seriousness of Adult Behavior
RGEOAF17   Adult Offense Seriousness/Intervention

Variables included for the regression on juvenile measures were pertinent to the juvenile period, while those included in the regression on adult measures could be for either the juvenile or adult period. The interview data (Table 5.2) accounted for far more of the variance in career seriousness for males than for females. Although more of the variance among Non-White females was accounted for than for Non-White males during the juvenile period, the opposite was found for the adult period, i.e., accounted for variance was greater for Non-White males than for Non-White females. More of the White male than White female variance was accounted for during both periods.

As juveniles, White male differences in official measures were best accounted for overall but the Non-White juvenile male differences in the

TABLE 5.2 VARIANCE ACCOUNTED FOR IN MEASURES OF JUVENILE AND ADULT OFFICIAL
SERIOUSNESS, SELF-REPORT SERIOUSNESS, AND OFFENSE SERIOUSNESS/
INTERVENTION SCORES BY INTERVIEW VARIABLES, BY RACE AND SEX

		Males	Non-White	White	Females	Non-White	White
Juvenile Measures							
JUVXN							
	R^2	.340*	.357ns	.388*	.185*	.473ns	.178*
Adj.	R^2	.314	.011	.360	.153	.200	.141
SRN617							
	R^2	.369*	.681*	.416*	.219*	.718*	.223*
Adj.	R^2	.344	.510	.389	.188	.571	.188
RGEOTH17							
	R^2	.372*	.443ns	.376*	.241*	.618*	.213*
Adj.	R^2	.347	.143	.347	.211	.419	.179
Adult Measures							
EIGHTPXN							
	R^2	.482*	.742*	.409*	.149*	.396ns	.207
Adj.	R^2	.458	.570	.377	.110	.001	.166
SRN18P							
	R^2	.335*	.715*	.332*	.172*	.568ns	.244*
Adj.	R^2	.304	.524	.296	.134	.287	.205
RGEOAF17							
	R^2	.365*	.560ns	.310*	.159*	.399ns	.141*
Adj.	R^2	.336	.266	.273	.120	.006	.097
N		361	40	321	364	38	326

* All R^2s in this table are marked "ns" if not significant at the .05 level o
by an "*" if significant at the .01 level or higher.

self-report measures were best accounted for. Female offense difference
were best accounted for among the Non-Whites during the juvenile perio
but best accounted for among the Whites during the adult period. Th
point is that controlling for sex and race/ethnicity vastly complexes an
attempt to account for differences in measures of delinquency and crime
While respectable amounts of the variation in delinquency and crim
measures are accounted for in several instances among race/ethnic groups
over half of the variance for the three measures is still unaccounted for i
most race/ethnic combinations.

Variables Utilized in Multiple Regression
Analyses for the Juvenile Period

Several interview variables used in Table 5.3 require more explanatio
than that provided thus far. INCHH is derived from "During the year
you were growing up, who was the income producing head of th
household?" The responses ranged from father or mother to anothe

TABLE 5.3 INTERVIEW VARIABLE EFFECTS ON MEASURES OF JUVENILE OFFICIAL
SERIOUSNESS, SELF-REPORT SERIOUSNESS, AND OFFENSE SERIOUSNESS/
INTERVENTION SCORES BY COHORT MEMBERS BY SEX AND RACE

	Males	Non-White	White	Females	Non-White	White
AGEDLR						
JUVXN	----	----	----	----	----	----
SRN617	-.108	----	-.120*	----	----	----
RGEOTH17	----	----	----	----	----	----
AGEMARRY						
JUVXN	----	----	----	----	----	----
SRN617	----	----	----	----	.294	----
RGEOTH17	----	----	----	----	----	----
INCHH						
JUVXN	----	----	----	----	----	----
SRN617	----	-.583*	----	----	----	----
RGEOTH17	----	----	----	----	----	----
HHEPMP						
JUVXN	-.127*	----	-.142*	-.229*	----	-.183*
SRN617	----	----	----	----	----	----
RGEOTH17	----	----	----	-.152*	----	-.134*
FIRSTJOB						
JUVXN	----	----	----	.117	----	.202*
SRN617	----	.303	----	----	----	----
RGEOTH17	----	----	----	----	----	.153*
JOBHSR						
JUVXN	-.102	----	-.099	----	----	.136
SRN617	----	----	----	.106	----	.111
RGEOTH17	-.131*	----	-.096	----	----	.115
ATTSCHR						
JUVXN	----	----	----	----	----	----
SRN617	----	.438*	----	----	----	----
RGEOTH17	----	----	----	----	----	----
NODIPLMR						
JUVXN	.273*	----	.283*	.133	----	.218*
SRN617	.236*	.366	.237*	----	----	----
RGEOTH17	.293*	----	.285*	.207*	----	.294*
ATTPOLR						
JUVXN	-.123	----	-.118	----	----	----
SRN617	-.149*	----	-.130*	----	-.285	----
RGEOTH17	-.134*	----	-.107	----	-.273	----
PATROLR						
JUVXN	----	----	----	----	----	----
SRN617	----	.282	----	----	----	----
RGEOTH17	----	----	----	----	----	----
SELF617						
JUVXN	----	----	.133*	----	----	----
SRN617	.231*	.488	.252*	.288*	.309	.277*
RGEOTH17	.117	----	.173*	----	----	.122
ADJFRTR						
JUVXN	.217*	----	.198*	.168*	.374	----
SRN617	.123	----	.252*	.122	.576*	----
RGEOTH17	.222*	----	.212*	.237*	.521*	----
ADAUTOSC						
JUVXN	.130*	----	.166*	----	----	----
SRN617	.204*	----	.226*	.225*	----	.238*
RGEOTH17	.161*	----	.161*	----	----	----

* All standardized estimates shown on this table are significant at the .05
level or, if followed by an *, at the .01 level or higher.

relative, stepparent, or foster parents. HHEMP is a dummy variable for that head's regularity of employment (regularly employed vs. not regularly employed).

Occupational level of respondent's first full time job is represented by FIRSTJOB and was coded into Professional, technical, managerial, proprietor, Clerical and sales, Craftsmen, foremen, Operatives, Maintenance and service, Private household labor, Industrial labor, and Farm labor. Respondent's high school employment (JOBHSR) is coded not employed, employed summers only, employed school year only, and employed summer and school year. Attitude toward high school, ATTSCHR, is a dummy variable and responses are negative vs. positive.

Since there were few high school drop-outs, responses to questions about achieved education were dichotomized to dropped out vs. graduated from high school. Attitude of respondent and closest friends toward police (as reported by respondent), ATTPOLR, has been recoded to negative, indifferent, or positive. Respondent's perception of how heavily his/her neighborhood had been patrolled during the juvenile years, PATROLR, presents responses as none, light, moderate, or heavy.

SELF617 is a measure of respondent's perception of his/her behavior as a juvenile and ranges from 1, non-delinquent, to 7, delinquent. ADJFRTR is an additive scale which measures respondent's friends trouble with the law during the juvenile period. It covers whether these friends had been questioned by the police, arrested, questioned and arrested, appeared in juvenile court (and any of the preceding), or been institutionalized (and any of the preceding). The scale order commences with questioning (the least serious) and ranges through levels of ascending seriousness to the level including the highest level of involvement.

The degree of auto use by respondent and friends as juveniles as described by respondent (ADAUTOSC) is an additive scale covering responses to questions about driving before obtaining a license without parental knowledge and consent, degree of access to a car while in high school, and time spent driving just for something to do. The scale ranges from 0, low auto use, to 3, high auto use.

Interview Variable Effects During the Juvenile Period: Race/Ethnicity and Sex

Although over one-third of the variance in male age period career seriousness (JUVXN) official and (SRN617) self-report scores was accounted for (Table 5.3), variable effects differed for the White/Non-White population from measure to measure. How the interview variables accounted for variation in Non-White vs. White male measures of delinquency and disproportional intervention (RGEOTH17) may be seen by noting where the significant effects appear in the standardized estimates. None of the interview variables had significant effects for Non-White males except when self-report seriousness was the dependent variable--where they were substantial for several variables. Non-White males are the only group for which the family structure, as defined by who was the income producing member of the family, was significantly related to a measure of delinquency, i.e., self-report seriousness, and here it was negative. This indicates that Non-White males with a father as income producing head of the household had higher self-report scores than if the mother was head of the household, all other things being equal, i.e., low-level first job, negative attitude toward school, failure to graduate from high school, living in an area heavily patrolled by police during junior high and high school, and a delinquent self-concept.

By contrast, the variables which have historically been related to delinquency, failure to graduate from high school, self-concept, friends in trouble with the police, and availability of an automobile, had significant effects on all measures of delinquency involvement for White males. Again, there were more significant effects for White females than for Non-White females but different from and still fewer than for White males. While there were few significant effects for the Non-White females, having juvenile friends in trouble with the police had effects on each of the delinquency measures.

It is interesting to note, for example, that the largest significant effects for either males or White males are found for NODIPLOMR, effects being similar for this variable on juvenile seriousness (JUVXN), juvenile self-report seriousness (SRN617), and juvenile disproportional intervention (RGEOTH17). That NODIPLOMR has no significant effects for Non-White male official offense measures points at differences in how the system works for Non-Whites and Whites. In other words, the value that has been attached to high school graduation has been based on White, middle-class experience, one that is not as available to Blacks. As we have suggested here and in other publications, an attempt to understand human behavior must consider differences in background and condition that vary sharply with race and ethnicity.

Interview Variable Effects During the Adult Period: Race/Ethnicity and Sex

Standardized estimates for the interview variable effects are presented for the adult period in Table 5.4. Two variables which have not been

TABLE 5.4 INTERVIEW VARIABLE EFFECTS ON MEASURES OF ADULT OFFICIAL SERIOUSNESS, SELF-REPORT SERIOUSNESS, AND OFFENSE SERIOUSNESS/INTERVENTION SCORES OF COHORT MEMBERS BY SEX AND RACE

	Males	Non-White	White	Females	Non-White	White
AGEDLR						
EIGHTPXN	----	-.360	----	-.138	----	----
SRN18P	-.114	-.330	-.106	-.112	----	----
RGEOAF17	----	----	----	-.123	----	----
AGEMARRY						
EIGHTPXN	.164*	----	.130	.120	----	.135
SRN18P	.144*	----	.144*	.166*	----	.182*
RGEOAF17	----	----	----	.144	----	.148
INCHH						
EIGHTPXN	----	----	----	----	----	----
SRN18P	----	----	----	.105	----	.112
RGEOAF17	.091	----	----	----	----	.116
HHEMP						
EIGHTPXN	-.182*	----	-.126	-.204*	----	-.280*
SRN18P	.122*	.434*	----	----	----	----
RGEOAF17	----	----	----	-.138*	----	-.186*
FIRSTJOB						
EIGHTPXN	.117*	.292	----	.157*	----	.108
SRN18P	----	.379	----	----	----	----
RGEOAF17	----	----	----	----	----	----
JOBHSR						
EIGHTPXN	-.085	----	----	----	----	----
SRN18P	----	----	----	----	----	----
RGEOAF17	----	----	----	----	----	----
ATTSCHR						
EIGHTPXN	.089	----	----	----	----	----
SRN18P	----	.454*	----	----	----	----
RGEOAF17	----	----	----	----	----	----
NODIPLMR						
EIGHTPXN	.362*	----	.412*	----	----	----
SRN18P	.180*	.461	.157*	----	----	----
RGEOAF17	.329*	----	.355*	.184*	----	.230*
ATTPOLR						
EIGHTPXN	-.114*	----	----	----	----	----
SRN18P	-.155*	----	-.150*	----	----	-.151*
RGEOAF17	-.152*	----	-.112	----	----	----
PATROLR						
EIGHTPXN	.106	.268	----	----	----	----
SRN18P	----	.273	----	-.124	----	-.147*
RGEOAF17	----	----	----	----	----	----
SELF617						
EIGHTPXN	----	----	.108	----	----	----
SRN18P	----	----	----	----	.359	----
RGEOAF17	----	----	----	----	----	----
ADJFRTR						
EIGHTPXN	----	----	----	----	----	----
SRN18P	.109	----	----	.105	.431	----
RGEOAF17	----	----	----	.127	----	----
ADAUTOSC						
EIGHTPXN	----	----	.117	-.123	----	----
SRN18P	.145*	----	.161*	.127	----	.131
RGEOAF17	.149*	----	.176*	----	----	----
MILITR						
EIGHTPXN	-.196*	----	-.143*	----	----	----
SRN18P	----	----	----	----	----	----
RGEOAF17	-.132	----	----	----	----	----
MARITAL						
EIGHTPXN	.232*	.394*	.201*	.221*	----	.313*
SRN18P	----	----	----	.149*	----	.227*
RGEOAF17	.157*	----	.141*	.187*	----	.155*
AFRDSCAL						
EIGHTPXN	.147*	----	.155*	----	----	----
SRN18P	.226*	----	.245*	.168*	----	.272*
RGEOAF17	----	----	----	----	----	----

* All standardized estimates shown on this table are significant at the .05 level or, if followed by an *, at the .01 level or higher.

previously described are included in this table. AFRDSCAL is the adult period equivalent to ADJFRTR. Respondent's marital status at the time of the interview (MARITAL) contains each reported status. The range is from never married to divorced, remarried, widowed.

While there are still fewer effects for the Non-Whites than for the Whites, the variance is again accounted for by a different pattern of significant effects than for the Whites. For example, NODIPLOMR, ADAUTOSC, MARITAL STATUS, and AFRDSCAL had more significant effects for Whites than for Non-Whites. There were very few significant effects for the Non-White females and, again, numerous significant effects for the White females.

Few variables had significant effects across sex, even fewer across race, and only one across sex and race for the juvenile period; there were more significant effects and more consistency across sex among Whites for the adult period, but still there was little consistency across race. Probably the most interesting finding was the continuing major effect of NODIPLOMR among males, particularly White males. This, of course, is not to say that failing to graduate from high school is in itself the variable which accounts for delinquency and crime more than any other variable, but it must be correlated with or indicative of a variable or variables which play an important part in the process of becoming delinquent or criminal. *We must conclude that the world of males differs from that of females and the world of Non-Whites differs from that of Whites when either juvenile delinquency or adult crime is related to interview data in all their complexity.*

Returning to the Inner City Neighborhoods

When all previous findings for these projects were taken into consideration, it again seemed appropriate to aggregate neighborhoods of socialization into inner city vs. others, partitioning cohort members in each by race/ethnicity and sex. More of the variance in the inner city delinquency and crime scores was generally accounted for by the interview variables (Table 5.5) than for those socialized in other neighborhoods. More of the variance for the Whites than the Non-Whites was accounted for during the juvenile period and the opposite was found for the adult period for official measures.

TABLE 5.5   VARIANCE ACCOUNTED FOR IN MEASURES OF JUVENILE AND ADULT OFFICIAL
            SERIOUSNESS, SELF-REPORT SERIOUSNESS, AND OFFENSE SERIOUSNESS/
            INTERVENTION SCORES BY INTERVIEW VARIABLES BY RESIDENCE AND SEX*

	Inner-City	Other	Non-White	White
JUVXN				
R^2	.416	.297	.359	.349
Adj. R^2	.365	.278	.221	.335
SRN617				
R^2	.387	.449	.497	.448
Adj. R^2	.333	.435	.388	.436
RGEOTH17				
R^2	.457	.392	.485	.394
Adj. R^2	.409	.376	.374	.380
EIGHTPXN				
R^2	.432	.341	.563	.291
Adj. R^2	.374	.321	.452	.274
SRN18P				
R^2	.419	.369	.477	.383
Adj. R^2	.360	.350	.345	.367
RGEOAF17				
R^2	.480	.290	.501 '	.296
Adj. R^2	.427	.268	.374	.278
N	174	552	79	647

* All R^2s in this table are significant at the .01 level or higher.

Interview Variable Effects During the Juvenile Period: Place of Residence and Sex

The significant standardized estimates for interview variable effects for various groupings of cohort members are presented in Table 5.6. There are inner city vs. other neighborhood and Non-White vs. White differences which are consistent with differences in the way of life of each group and other neighborhood vs. White similarities because other neighborhoods are predominantly White. For example, not having graduated from high school and having access to an automobile while a juvenile have significant effects for Whites but not for Non-Whites. The importance of these variables was also greater for persons residing outside the inner city than for those from the inner city. Having friends in trouble with the police had significant effects on each group.

TABLE 5.6   INTERVIEW VARIABLE EFFECTS ON MEASURES OF JUVENILE OFFICIAL
SERIOUSNESS, SELF-REPORT SERIOUSNESS, AND OFFENSE
SERIOUSNESS/INTERVENTION SCORES BY COHORT MEMBERS BY SEX AND RACE

	Inner-City	Other	Non-White	White
AGEDLR				
JUVXN	----	----	----	----
SRN617	----	----	----	----
RGEOTH17	----	----	----	----
AGEMARRY				
JUVXN	----	----	----	----
SRN617	----	.071	----	----
RGEOTH17	----	----	----	----
INCHH				.076
JUVXN	----	----	----	
SRN617	----	----	-.389*	----
RGEOTH17	----	----	----	----
HHEMP				-.113*
JUVXN	-.244*	----	----	
SRN617	----	----	----	----
RGEOTH17	-.168*	----	----	----
FIRSTJOB				
JUVXN	----	----	----	----
SRN617	----	----	.235	----
RGEOTH17	.147	----	----	----
JOBHSR				
JUVXN	----	----	----	----
SRN617	----	.082	----	.087*
RGEOTH17	-.139	----	----	----
ATTSCHR				
JUVXN	----	----	----	----
SRN617	----	----	----	----
RGEOTH17	----	----	----	----
NODIPLMR				
JUVXN	.182*	.195*	----	.218*
SRN617	----	.132*	----	.143*
RGEOTH17	.127	.257*	----	.230*
ATTPOLR				
JUVXN	-.173	----	----	-.087
SRN617	-.218*	-.077	-.218	-.087*
RGEOTH17	-.164	-.095	-.286*	-.075
PATROLR				.068
JUVXN	----	----	----	
SRN617	----	----	----	----
RGEOTH17	----	----	----	----
SELF617				
JUVXN	----	.140*	----	.163*
SRN617	.210*	.269*	.382*	.274*
RGEOTH17	----	.204*	----	.196*
ADJFRTR				
JUVXN	.216*	.211*	.324*	.230*
SRN617	----	.176*	----	.148*
RGEOTH17	.305*	.177*	.378*	.221*
ADAUTOSC				
JUVXN	.171	.095	----	.142
SRN617	.173	.223*	----	.222*
RGEOTH17	.206*	.147*	----	.156*
MILITR				----
JUVXN	----	.109*	----	.135*
SRN617	----	.108*	----	.084
RGEOTH17	----	.094	----	

* All standardized estimates shown on this table are significant at the .05
level or, if followed by an *, at the .01 level or higher.

TABLE 5.7 INTERVIEW VARIABLE EFFECTS ON MEASURES OF ADULT OFFICIAL SERIOUSNESS, SELF-REPORT SERIOUSNESS, AND OFFENSE SERIOUSNESS/INTERVENTION SCORES OF COHORT MEMBERS RESIDENT IN INNER CITY VS. OTHER NEIGHBORHOODS AND NON-WHITE VS. WHITE COHORT MEMBERS

	Inner-City	Other	Non-White	White
AGEDLR				
EIGHTPXN	-.207*	----	-.279*	----
SRN18P	----	-.074	----	-.085
RGEOAF17	-.212*	----	-.326*	----
AGEMARRY				
EIGHTPXN	.236*	.127*	----	.155*
SRN18P	----	.198*	----	.156*
RGEOAF17	.181*	.115*	----	.129*
INCHH				
EIGHTPXN	----	----	----	.078
SRN18P	----	----	----	.071
RGEOAF17	----	.091	----	.077
HHEMP				
EIGHTPXN	-.167	-.157*	-.221	-.187*
SRN18P	----	----	----	----
RGEOAF17	----	----	----	----
FIRSTJOB				
EIGHTPXN	.213*	.112*	.226	.088
SRN18P	.165	----	.240	----
RGEOAF17	.185*	.084	----	.077
JOBHSR				
EIGHTPXN	----	----	----	----
SRN18P	----	----	----	----
RGEOAF17	----	----	----	----
ATTSCHR				
EIGHTPXN	----	----	----	----
SRN18P	----	----	----	----
RGEOAF17	.171*	----	----	----
NODIPLMR				
EIGHTPXN	.140	.361*	----	.254*
SRN18P	.137	.083	----	.073
RGEOAF17	----	.285*	----	.249*
ATTPOLR				
EIGHTPXN	----	----	----	----
SRN18P	-.168	-.136*	----	-.146*
RGEOAF17	-.183*	-.085	-.220	----
PATROLR				
EIGHTPXN	----	----	.194	----
SRN18P	----	----	----	----
RGEOAF17	----	----	----	----
SELF617				
EIGHTPXN	----	----	----	.186*
SRN18P	----	.085	----	.085
RGEOAF17	----	----	----	.134*
ADJFRTR				
EIGHTPXN	----	----	----	----
SRN18P	----	.150*	----	.096*
RGEOAF17	.239*	----	.213	----
ADAUTOSC				
EIGHTPXN	----	----	----	----
SRN18P	----	.152*	----	.157*
RGEOAF17	----	.140*	----	.128*
MILITR				
EIGHTPXN	-.252*	----	----	----
SRN18P	----	----	----	.072
RGEOAF17	----	----	----	----
MARITAL				
EIGHTPXN	.133	.163*	----	.158*
SRN18P	----	.130*	----	.116*
RGEOAF17	.154	----	----	.099*
AFRDSCAL				
EIGHTPXN	.272*	.234*	----	.206*
SRN18P	.308*	.188*	----	.252*
RGEOAF17	.136	.127*	----	.100*

* All standardized estimates shown on this table are significant at the .05 level or, if followed by an *, at the .01 level or higher.

Interview Variable Effects During the Adult Period:
Place of Residence and Sex

The interview variable effects on adult measures are presented in Table 5.7. Note that the sex or relationship of the income producing head of the household to the respondent carried no significant effects into adult crime for persons socialized in the inner city or for Non-Whites but that regularity of employment of the head of the household in which the juvenile was socialized tended to reduce delinquency seriousness scores in all groups, as did a high-level first job of cohort members for all groups except the Whites. High-level first job had substantial positive correlations for all measures in all groups at the zero-order level, particularly for Non-Whites. Not graduating from high school had its greatest effects on Whites and those who were socialized outside the inner city. This is, of course, consistent with the findings presented in Tables 5.6 and 5.7.

Having adult friends in trouble with the police had few significant relationships to offense rates in the multiple regression analysis, although at the zero-order level the relationship for Non-Whites had been presentand essentially the same as having juvenile friends in trouble with the police. What this means is that having adult friends in trouble with the police may be no reflection on one's own behavior but is the baggage that one carries as a member of the group. In fact, at the zero-order level these variables and failure to graduate from high school had the highest relationships with measures of adult crime for all groups.

Marital status of cohort members had significant effects for Whites or those residing in non-inner city neighborhoods, i.e., any status such as divorced or separated had a significant positive effect on adult offense measures. However, it is difficult to say that marital status caused criminal behavior (the lack of marriage is the removal of a social control) because it may well be that persons involved in crime were separated from or divorced by their predominantly female and wiser spouses.

One could, after the fact, write an entire volume on how the results of these multiple regression analyses are supportive of sociological theory and various hypotheses derived from this or that theory or the process by which delinquent and criminal behavior patterns are acquired. We would, however, prefer to say at this point that it is even more obvious than before that the organization of human relations differs between the inner city and other types of neighborhoods. It is a question of how the development of delinquency and crime differs and is dealt with differently depending on the type of neighborhood in which the juvenile has been socialized. There are not only differences in the extent to which the interview variables account for measures of official and self-report delinquency and crime but there are also very significant differences in the extent to which they account for the offense seriousness/intervention measure which incorporates society's reaction to delinquency and crime. Thus, we must be even more concerned about how the decision-making process operates differently for persons in some neighborhoods from the way it operates for persons in others.

Parallel to this is the question of race/ethnic differences. Is there an added impact of some variables if the juvenile or adult is a Non-White, inner city resident? For example, why did attitude toward the police have a significant standardized estimate in accounting for variation in offense seriousness/intervention scores for Non-Whites but not for Whites during the juvenile period? Why was it greater for Non-Whites than for all inner city residents?

Summarizing the Variance Accounted For

Having created fairly homogeneous groups by controlling for place of residence, race, and sex, as shown in Table 5.8, a major summary table for this stage of the Racine research, brought us to the point that from half to three-fourths of the variance in both official adult crime rates and self-report rates among inner city Non-White and White males had been accounted for by type of associates, life experiences, attitudes, living arrangements, and juvenile police record. This set the stage for understanding the settings in which and processes by which people continue in delinquency and proceed to adult crime.

More of the variance in both of these measures of adult seriousness was accounted for among inner city males, White or Non-White, and least among White females from either the inner city or other neighborhoods. This, however, was not the case for offense/seriousness disproportional intervention scores where there was less success in accounting for variation among inner city Non-White males, even with the juvenile disproportional intervention scores added.

That the standardized estimates for variables such as failure to graduate from high school, juvenile friends in trouble with the police, and access to an automobile while in high school differed from group to group when included in multiple regression analyses suggested that the chain of experiences through which juveniles acquired a given level of official seriousness, self-report seriousness, and offense seriousness/intervention scores had only limited group to group similarity. Unstandardized estimates indicated that the size of the effects of the independent variables on measures of delinquency and crime were quite different across groups.

TABLE 5.8   VARIANCE IN MEASURES OF JUVENILE DELINQUENCY ACCOUNTED FOR BY
INTERVIEW VARIABLES AND ADULT CRIME ACCOUNTED FOR BY INTERVIEW
VARIABLES AND JUVENILE MEASURES

	Inner City Non-White Males	Inner City White Males	Other White Males	Inner City Non-White Females	Inner City White Females	Other White Females
Juvenile Measures						
JUVXN						
R^2	.455ns	.593*	.398*	.571ns	.359ns	.225*
Adj. R^2	.000	.487	.363	.222	.081	.184
SRN617						
R^2	.916*	.410*	.451*	.825*	.429ns	.218*
Adj. R^2	.843	.257	.419	.683	.181	.177
RGEOTH17						
R^2	.510ns	.512*	.378*	.779*	.464ns	.247*
Adj. R^2	.081	.386	.341	.599	.232	.207
Adult Measures						
EIGHTPXN						
R^2	.762	.609	.426	.570	.471ns	.189
Adj. R^2	.490	.488	.387	.110	.187	.140
JUVXN SE **	.506*	.760*	.426*	.691	-.091ns	.028ns
R^2	.869*	.795*	.534*	.731ns	.475ns	.189*
Adj. R^2	.697	.727	.501	.399	.164	.137
SRN18P						
R^2	.895	.468	.383	.717	.498ns	.242
Adj. R^2	.774	.304	.341	.414	.229	.196
SRN617 SE **	.645ns	.520*	.361*	.496ns	-.098ns	.389*
R^2	.887*	.627*	.454*	.754ns	.502ns	.354*
Adj. R^2	.740	.502	.414	.451	.207	.312
RGEOAF17						
R^2	.598	.550	.318	.589	.446ns	.128
Adj. R^2	.138	.412	.272	.149	.149	.076
RGEOTH17 SE **	.350ns	.377*	.392*	.897*	-.031ns	.119ns
R^2	.646ns	.610*	.413*	.744ns	.444ns	.138*
Adj. R^2	.183	.480	.370	.430	.119	.083
N	31	69	252	30	45	282

** These are the standardized estimates for juvenile measures included as
independent variables in the regression analyses. All standardized estimates and
R^2s in this table are marked "ns" if not significant at the .05 level or by an "*"
significant at the .01 level or higher.

This left us with the conclusion that the social processes that lead to delinquency and crime operate differently in different contexts and for different race/ethnic and sex groups. This is not new to us and should not be new to anyone who has conducted research with sizeable samples of birth cohorts. The relationship between educational attainment and a variety of other mobility measures has long been known to vary by race/ethnicity and sex.

In sum, accounting for either juvenile delinquency or adult crime was a difficult enterprise but, when the group was partitioned by race/ethnicity and inner city vs. other places of juvenile residence, 70% of the adult offense seriousness for inner city Non-White males was accounted for by juvenile seriousness and the interview variables. It was 73% for inner city White males and declined to 14% for White females from non-inner city neighborhoods. The proportion of the disproportional intervention accounted for among inner city Non-Whites was only 18% compared to 48% for inner city Whites.

The question still remains, aside from the fact that variance in the independent variables (the variables that affect delinquency rates) is greater for inner city males and other males, why are variable effects more pronounced for males in terms of offense seriousness but less pronounced for disproportional intervention? It is our suspicion that the interview variables and other variables which account for considerable amounts of official and self-report delinquency and crime do not account for disproportional intervention because disproportional intervention is explained by a different set of variables which are internal to judges but which have a reasonable rationale to them in the process of decision-making. Now we are ready to look into the future and perhaps surprising effects of sanctions on continuity in delinquency and crime.

Chapter 6

A MORE PRECISE EVALUATION OF THE EFFECTS OF SANCTIONS

Introduction to the Fourth Project

Offense seriousness has a very volatile quality even among serious career offenders. Although there are continuities in delinquency and crime, what a person will do next after any contact or after all prior contacts is not predictable. This is why the police, probation, court workers, judges, parole boards, etc., have so much difficulty. Furthermore, the assumption that how persons on the firing line deal with miscreants enables them or others to predict what the offender will do next is probably the most fallible.

Our previously reported findings that efforts aimed at specific and general deterrence didn't seem to work in Racine, findings paralleling the more general conclusions of Martinson (1974), Hopkins (1976), and Greenberg (1978), should not have been too surprising. With controls for offense seriousness (felonies vs. misdemeanors or Part I vs. others) and juvenile vs. adult offender status, there was no uniformity in severity of dispositions or severity of sanctions. Whether there should be uniformity has always been a debatable question because juvenile courts in particular are expected to take background factors and the circumstances surrounding misbehavior into consideration in determining the disposition of cases. With controls for cohort, except for an overall increase in severity of dispositions, particularly for more serious juvenile offenses, there were no consistent trends. Either general or specific deterrence theories would suggest a decline or at least a leveling off of the seriousness of individual careers of persons who were sanctioned and a decline in total offense frequency and seriousness over the years. The cohort and age period data did not show this.

We were, however, concerned that age period data for the three birth cohorts, i.e., cumulated frequency, offense seriousness, referral, and severity of sanctions data, had not enabled us to arrive at a sufficiently definitive assessment of the effects of sanctions, particularly as they related to and varied with offense seriousness.[1] The fourth stage of our

Racine research involved a recoding of severity of sanctions as matched to specific offenses, offense by offense, as a basis for more definitive tests of the effects of sanctions as applied. Evaluating the findings in a study of this nature is not easy because offenses and efforts to reduce their frequency and seriousness through intervention and more severe sanctioning do not take place in a vacuum. At the same time that disposition and sanctioning policies may call for increasingly severe sanctions, the population composition may be changing because opportunities for employment have increased in the community. On the other hand, structural changes, changes in the organization of production, for example, may reduce the need for unskilled and relatively inexperienced labor. Thus, in any given neighborhood the impact of social and structural changes may be greater than the effects of ongoing social processes. Both may be overshadowed by the effects of social conflict.

Beyond the literature cited, the effects of extra-legal and other complicating factors determining the severity of sanctions have been illuminated by McEachern and Bauzer (1967), Black (1970), Arnold (1971), Chiricos, Jackson, and Waldo (1972), Thornberry (1973), Tittle and Logan (1973), Liska and Tausig (1974), Thomas and Cage (1977), Gibbs (1977), Greenberg, Kessler, and Logan (1979), and Unnever, Frazier, and Henretta (1980). Most recently, the complexity of the research problem has been delineated by Blumstein, Cohen, Martin, and Tonry (1983). One should not, of course, expect any consistent findings in the sanctioning literature considering the differences in sentencing for the same offense within and across jurisdictions (Greenwood, Abrahamse, and Zimring, 1984). The controversy also indicates that conclusions should not be drawn from the fact that extra-legal variables may not have statistical significance in cross-sectional studies at specific points in time or careers.

Extra-legal variables are most likely to have significance in a longitudinal study if the effects of being Non-White, living in Inner City or Transitional neighborhoods, and having a lower SES background have had an opportunity to accumulate. Their effects will remain and, for some, increase even though seriousness of present offense and prior record of sanctions may invariably have the greatest weight in determining the decision to refer either a juvenile or an adult (Thornberry and Christianson, 1984).

In the Racine case, for example, when severity of present sanction was regressed on such variables as seriousness of present offense, total prior offense seriousness, severity of prior sanctions, juvenile neighborhood, sex, race, and age at contact for the first ten police contacts by Racine cohort members, *seriousness of present offense* was most frequently followed by *severity of prior sanctions* at the juvenile level as the determinant of the severity of the present sanction. Total prior adult seriousness also out-weighed severity of prior sanctions until the seventh police contact.

When juvenile and adult careers were combined the dominance of juvenile careers produced results for the total that were similar to the juvenile results, suggesting that, however inconsistent dispositions and sanctions may be, they play a part in what will happen to an offender in future court appearances. What some allude to as the whimsical nature of sentencing was brought out by the fact that at no time from the first through the tenth police contact was more than 20% of the severity of sanctions accounted for. Yet, four out of five juveniles who had non-traffic police contacts before the age of 18 ceased, as adults, to commit acts which brought them into contact with the police. In the next section we shall take a close look at the effects of sanctions on career continuity in Racine.

Concentration on Cohort Members with Non-Traffic Contacts, Ages 13-22

Persons from the combined cohorts who had non-traffic police contacts ages 13-22 are aggregated into two-year periods in Table 6.1. Each of the 1,798 offenders who had one of the thirty-one types of careers is arrayed from the 153 with at least one non-traffic contact ages 13-14 to the 107 with at least one such contact ages 21-22. There were only 201 (less than 5% of the total) persons who had no non-traffic police contacts ages 13-22 but had one or more at a younger or older age. There were 602 with only traffic contacts at any age and 1,478 who never had a police contact. Table 6.1 dramatizes how varied and complex careers were for even such a short span of time.

The complexity of the delinquency/crime experience patterns that we have attempted to encapsulate is further demonstrated by Diagram 6.1. Cohort members drifted in and out of delinquency and/or crime, making the analysis quite complex. If the last stage (21-23) had been presented we would have included 107 persons who had not had a non-traffic contact since age 12 and would have lost 352 persons who had contacts at ages 19-20 but did not have a contact during ages 21-22.

Statistics from collapsed data usually produce somewhat lower correlations than do uncollapsed data but tables derived from uncollapsed data do not enable the reader to follow the discussion of relationships as

TABLE 6.1   CONTINUITY TYPES OF DELINQUENT AND YOUNG ADULT CAREERS BASED ON NON-TRAFFIC POLICE CONTACTS, BY TWO-YEAR PERIODS, FOR COMBINED COHORTS*

Types	Age 13-14	Age 15-16	Age 17-18	Age 19-20	Age 21-22	NUMBER
1	X					153
2	X	X				75
3	X	X	X			83
4	X	X	X	X		57
5	X	X	X	X	X	85
6	X	X	X		X	36
7	X	X		X	X	20
8	X	X			X	13
9	X	X		X		24
10	X		X	X	X	7
11	X		X	X		15
12	X		X		X	8
13	X		X			38
14	X			X	X	15
15	X			X		24
16	X				X	11
17		X				234
18		X	X			93
19		X	X	X		40
20		X	X	X	X	51
21		X	X		X	28
22		X		X	X	11
23		X		X		41
24		X			X	28
25			X			201
26			X	X		50
27			X	X	X	22
28			X		X	32
29				X		151
30				X	X	45
31					X	107
32	No Non-Traffic Contacts 13-22					201
33	Traffic Contacts only During Entire Career					602
34	No Contacts at Any Time During Career					1478
TOTAL	664	919	846	658	519	4079

*   Cohort members had at least one non-traffic contact during the age period.

readily. Contacts for minor misdemeanors and major misdemeanors were, therefore, collapsed as non-felony contacts for Tables 6.2 and 6.3, thus reducing the categories to a point where one could readily detect trends and relationships. These tables are followed by a description of several multivariate analyses in which some of the independent variables and the dependent variables (future offense seriousness) are utilized in uncollapsed form, i.e., as continuous variables.

An Overview of Age Periods

Table 6.2 is based on those who had any non-traffic police contacts (referred to as No Contact in the tables), age period by age period, and characterizes offenders by the most serious offense that each had during

DIAGRAM 6.1 CONTINUITY AND DISCONTINUITY FOR PERSONS WITH NON-TRAFFIC POLICE
CONTACTS, AGES 13-20, FOR COMBINED COHORTS

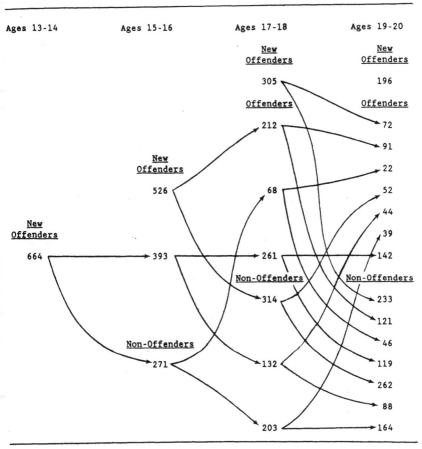

Ages 13-14   Ages 15-16   Ages 17-18   Ages 19-20

each two-year period. The percent whose most serious police contacts
consisted of referred felony-level offenses reached its peak at ages 15-20,
15.8%, 16.3%, and 16.2% (see subtotal for Felony Referred). They
comprised only 3.6%, 3.4%, and 2.6% of the combined cohorts, i.e.,
3.6% of the combined cohort members had referred felony-level contacts
at ages 15 or 16, 3.4% at 17 or 18, and 2.6% at ages 19 or 20, a very
small proportion of the youth of those ages. That about half of those with
referred felony-level offenses received a dismissal and relatively few were
institutionalized may be of concern in one respect to those who believe
that we are too easy on youth but, on the other hand, a concern of those
who believe that only a small proportion of the youthful offenders who are
referred should be dealt with by formal court sanctions.

TABLE 6.2   DISPOSITION OF THEIR MOST SERIOUS NON-TRAFFIC POLICE CONTACTS FOR COMBINED COHORT MEMBERS, AGES 13 THROUGH 22, BY TWO-YEAR PERIODS*

	Age 13-14		Age 15-16		Age 17-18		Age 19-20		Age 21-22	
	N	%	N	%	N	%	N	%	N	%
Contact Not Referred	451	67.9	515	56.0	439	51.9	382	58.1	355	68.4
Non-Felony Referral										
Dismissed	117	17.6	202	22.0	189	23.3	87	13.2	54	10.4
Fined			10	1.1	51	6.0	65	9.9	52	10.0
Probation	16	2.4	40	4.4	18	2.1	3	.5	1	.2
Institutionalized			7	.8	11	1.3	14	2.1	9	1.7
Subtotal	133	20.0	259	28.3	269	31.8	169	25.7	116	22.4
Felony Referral										
Dismissed	38	5.7	70	7.6	80	9.5	58	8.8	34	6.6
Fined			5	.5	9	1.1	13	2.0	4	.7
Probation	32	4.8	44	4.8	30	3.5	21	3.2	5	1.0
Institutionalized	10	1.5	26	2.8	19	2.2	15	2.3	5	1.0
Subtotal	80	12.0	145	15.8	138	16.3	107	16.2	48	9.2
TOTAL	664	99.9	919	100.0	846	100.0	658	100.0	519	100.0

* If a cohort member had more than one police contact during any two-year period, the most serious was selected, and if there were two of equal seriousness, the one receiving the most severe disposition was selected

Beginning and Following Age Periods

Commencing at Ages 13-14. We next examined the status of offenders at the two-year age period of 13-14 and at each following two-year age period, as shown in Table 6.3. The Ns at the right hand side of each segment of the table correspond to the appropriate Ns for ages 13-14 *in that table* (this does not include the No Contact either age period category, which increased in number from 2,905 at ages 13-14 and 15-16 to 3,008 for the ages 19-20 and 21-22). Several persons from each panel were also eliminated because their categories were so small that there would have been unnecessary cluttering in the four panels of the table. The percentages for each of the ages 13-14 categories are shown as are the Ns and percentages of each offense and dispositional category for each age period beyond ages 13-14.

The marginals assist us in describing categorical change (what went on inside of each age segment of the table). By reading across each row of each age segment of the table (omitting the subtables) one may observe how the persons in each of the five categories at the left of the table at ages 13-14 were distributed at ages 15-16, 17-18, 19-20, and 21-22. These distributions differ in following age periods on a basis of the behavior of cohort members and how society had responded to their behavior in the previous age period. For example, 47.5% of the 451 with unreferred contacts at ages of 13-14, had no police contacts at ages 15-16. This increased to 72.5% at ages 21-22. And, although 27.5% of the 451 had an unreferred non-traffic contact at ages 15-16, this had declined to 17.3% by ages 21-22. Similarly, if one examines the 117 cohort members in the Non-Felony Referred: Dismissed category for ages 13-14, one finds an increase in the percent with no contact from age period to age period, 36.8% to 74.4%.

Overall, the figures in the No Contact (left hand column of Table 6.3) indicate that *within* each two-year tables from 15-16, 17-18, 19-20, and 21-22 there was a general decline in the percent who had no contact in the following age period, starting with the 451 with unreferred contacts and ending with the ten who had referred felonies resulting in institutionalization (i.e., 47.5% to .0%, 54.1% to 10.0%, 67.9% to 20.0%, 72.5% to 60.0%). Thus, the undesirable effects of early institutionalization seemed to wear off slowly compared to the effects of probation or dismissal.

As one proceeds from having a non-referred contact to a felony contact culminating in institutionalization, the percent who had at least one felony referral in the next two-year period tends to increase within each two-year segment of the table. These figures are in the vertical boxes.

TABLE 6.3 STATUS OF COMBINED COHORT MEMBERS ACCORDING TO DISPOSITION OF THEIR MOST SERIOUS NON-TRAFFIC POLICE CONTACT AT AGES 13-14 BY SUBSEQUENT TWO-YEAR PERIODS*

STATUS AGES 13-14 — STATUS AGES 15-16

	No Cont	No Ref	Non-Felony Referred					Felony Referred					N	%
			Dism	Fine	Prob	Inst	Sub-Tot	Dism	Fine	Prob	Inst	Sub-Tot		
No Contact	----	65.2	22.4	.9	3.0	.6	26.9	4.4	.4	2.7	.4	7.9	526	44.8
Contact Not Referred	47.5	27.5	10.9	.9	3.1	.4	15.3	4.4	.4	2.7	2.2	9.7	451	38.4
Non-Felony Referred: Dismissed	36.8	27.4	12.8	.9	4.3	1.7	19.8	6.8	.9	7.7	.9	16.3	117	10.0
Felony Referred: Dismissed	21.1	13.2	21.1	---	5.3	---	26.4	23.7	---	5.3	10.5	39.5	38	3.2
Probation	15.6	25.0	21.9	---	3.1	---	25.0	18.8	---	6.3	9.4	34.5	32	2.7
Institutionalized	----	20.0	20.0	---	---	---	20.0	20.0	---	---	40.0	60.0	10	.9
TOTAL: N	270	514	199	10	38	7	254	68	5	39	24	136	1174	
%	23.0	43.8	17.0	.9	3.2	.6	21.6	5.8	.4	3.3	2.0	11.6		100.0

STATUS AGES 13-14 — STATUS AGES 17-18

	No Cont	No Ref	Non-Felony Referred					Felony Referred					N	%
			Dism	Fine	Prob	Inst	Sub-Tot	Dism	Fine	Prob	Inst	Sub-Tot		
No Contact	----	56.9	22.6	6.2	2.3	.8	31.9	8.5	1.0	1.4	.4	11.3	517	44.3
Contact Not Referred	54.1	22.8	10.2	2.9	.7	1.3	15.1	3.3	.9	2.2	1.6	8.0	451	38.7
Non-Felony Referred: Dismissed	50.4	20.5	10.3	3.4	.9	---	14.6	6.0	---	6.8	1.7	14.5	117	10.0
Felony Referred: Dismissed	31.6	26.3	10.5	2.6	2.6	2.6	18.3	15.8	---	---	7.9	23.7	38	3.3
Probation	46.9	12.5	15.6	---	---	---	15.6	12.5	---	6.3	6.3	25.1	32	2.7
Institutionalized	10.0	30.0	10.1	10.0	---	---	20.0	20.0	---	10.0	10.0	40.0	10	.9
TOTAL: N	331	438	185	51	17	11	264	78	9	28	17	132	1165	
%	28.4	37.6	15.9	4.4	1.5	.9	22.7	6.7	.8	2.4	1.5	11.3		100.0

S T A T U S   A G E S   1 3 - 1 4 | **S T A T U S   A G E S   1 9 - 2 0**

Disposition	13-14		19-20							Total	
	N/%	…	N/%							N	%
No Contact	---- / 67.9		10.4 / 6.9	.2 / .2	1.7 / .4	6.6 / 4.2	1.2 / .7	2.4 / .9	.2 / 1.1	411	38.8
Contact Not Referred	64.5 / 18.4	13.6 / 3.6	9.5 / 2.7	.2 / .2	1.7 / .4	25.1 / 6.9	6.6 / 4.2	1.2 / .7	2.4 / .9	451	42.6
Non-Felony Referred:											
Dismissed	61.6 / 14.5	7.7 / 5.1	.9	1.7	15.4	3.4	2.6		8.6	117	11.0
Felony Referred:											
Dismissed	47.4 / 7.9	2.6 / 7.9	7.9 / 6.3	----	7.9	18.4 / 15.7	10.5 / 3.1	2.6 / 3.1	5.3 / 3.1	26.3 / 12.4	38	3.6
Probation	50.0 / 21.9	9.4 / 6.3	----	----	----	15.7 / 10.0	3.1	3.1	3.1	38?	32	3.0
Institutionalized	20.0 / 30.0	10.0	----	----	10.0	20.0	----	----	20.0	40.0	10	0.9
TOTAL: N	414	378	86	62	14	165	57	13	17	15	102	1059
%	39.1	35.7	8.1	5.9	1.3	15.6	5.4	1.2	1.6	1.4	9.6	100.0

S T A T U S   A G E S   1 3 - 1 4 | **S T A T U S   A G E S   2 1 - 2 2**

Disposition	13-14		21-22						Total	
	N/%	…	N/%						N	%
No Contact	---- / 72.5		4.6 / 1.8	.3	.3	1.2 / .9	19.4 / 7.3	4.6 / 1.8	324	33.3
Contact Not Referred	74.4 / 17.3	10.5 / 3.1	7.7 / 3.3	---- / .2	.9	1.2 / .9	7.3	.3 / .7	451	46.3
Non-Felony Referred:										
Dismissed	74.4	11.9	2.6	6.0	.9	9.5	2.6	1.7	4.3	117 / 12.0
Felony Referred:										
Dismissed	50.0 / 29.0	5.3 / 3.1	5.3 / 3.1	2.6	13.2 / 6.2	5.3 / 9.4	----	2.6	7.9 / 9.4	38 / 3.9
Probation	59.4 / 25.0	3.1	3.1	----	6.2	9.4	----	----	20.0	32 / 3.3
Institutionalized	60.0 / 20.0	----	----	----	----	----	20.0	----	20.0	10 / 1.0
TOTAL: N	458	354	54	50	9	116	33			974
%	47.0	36.3	5.5	5.1	.9	11.9	3.4			100.0

* Categories of dispositions other than dismissal are eliminated for misdemeanor or lesser offenses and fines for felony-level offenses for Status Ages 13-14 because there were fewer than ten persons in each.

In other words, institutionalization for a felony was more likely to have as its consequence another felony than were less punitive responses. As high as 60% of those who were institutionalized (six out of ten at ages 15-16) behaved in the next age period in such a way as to have at least one other felony referral on their records.

More important, however, is the fact that the percent with referred felonies during ages 13-14 who, in the next age period, had referred felonies, varied depending upon whether the referred felony had been dealt with by a dismissal, by probation, or by institutionalization. This is also shown for each following age period in the vertical boxes in Table 6.3.

When the expected figures were computed for each cell of the table based on the marginals, there were invariably more persons in the age 13-14 Contact but Not Referred and Dismissed columns who had No Contacts during the following age periods than expected. At the opposite corner of each segment of the table, those with Referred Felonies who had been institutionalized, there were more who had Referred Felonies in the following period than expected, but the pattern was not as consistent or clear cut.

Commencing at Ages 15-16. Since ages 13-14 might be considered too early for the first two years of such an analysis, we constructed the same set of tables for those who had had non-traffic police contacts at ages 15-16 (not included). This set of tables and the findings described on the following pages also facilitate comparison of all adjacent age periods, e.g., 15-16 with 17-18, 17-18 with 19-20, etc. These may or may not be the same persons as those included in Table 6.3. Some, of course, had contacts at both ages 13-14 and 15-16 (393). Those who had contacts at 13-14 but not at 15-16 are not included in this stage of the analysis (271) but those who were not in Table 6.3 but did have contacts at 15-16 are added (526). Persons with referred felonies during ages 15-16 had declines in their percent with referred felonies ages 17-18, 19-20, and 21-22 somewhat more immediately after the initial period but to essentially the same extent by ages 21-22 as did those who had their first contacts at ages 13-14. The most important point is that *persons with referred felonies resulting in institutionalization were again more likely to have referred felonies in the following period than were those whose referred felonies had resulted in less severe sanctions.*

Commencing at Ages 17-18 and 19-20. The population of this group differed from the previous two age groups in the same kinds of ways (but more complicated) that the ages 15-16 group differed from the ages 13-14 group. Over 300 cohort members are added for ages 17-18 but 649 desisted for at least two years (see Diagram 6.1). There was a rise in percent with no contacts in ages 19-20 and 21-22 and a relatively lower percent with further referred felonies from each group with earlier referred felonies (17-18). Institutionalization of persons with felony contacts at later ages does not seem to produce proportionately as many with felony contacts at following ages as it does for persons institutionalized at earlier ages. In other words, nipping them in the bud (early institutionalization) had more deleterious effects in the years which followed than did later institutionalization.

Comparison of Analyses Based on Different Ages

In Table 6.3 we noted that of those who had a Contact Not Referred ages 13-14, 47.5% had No Contacts at ages 15-16, this percent increasing to 72.5% by ages 21-22. Those who had a Contact Not Referred ages 15-16, 63.9% had No Contacts 17-18, 61.7% and 58.9% had none in the two following age periods. That group who had a Contact Not Referred ages 13-14 had 54.1% with No Contacts at ages 17-18 while the comparable figure for those with a Contact Not Referred ages 15-16 was 61.7%. Those who had No Contacts at ages 17-18 had 59.0% with No Contacts at ages 19-20 and 55.6% at the following ages. In sum, *the proportion who had No Contacts in the following age periods was generally higher if the analysis was based on those who had police contacts at later ages, whether those included in the first age period of the comparison were involved in their first or Nth contact.*

We are, however, more concerned about those segments of each table which show the relationship of persons who had referred felony-level police contacts at ages 13-14, 15-16, etc., to their status at following age periods. There were eighty such persons at ages 13-14, 145 at 15-16, 138 at 17-18, and 107 at 19-20. Among those with felony-level referrals at ages 13-14 who were institutionalized, the percentages with felony-level referrals in the succeeding age periods were 60%, 40%, 40%, and 20%. When all persons with felony-level referrals at ages 15-16 who were institutionalized were considered, the continued felony referral rates were 54%, 39%, and 8%. Only 26% and 5% of the persons institutionalized for felony-level referrals at ages 17-18 and 7% at ages 19-20 had felony-level referrals in the following age periods. As we have said before, the rate of decline was slower depending upon offense seriousness and severity of disposition. For example, those who received probation for a felony-level referral at ages 13-14 had following felony-level referral rates of 84%, 25%, 12%, and 9%. Dismissal as a disposition had following felony-level referral rates of 40%, 24%, 26%, and 8%.

Although there was no control for length of institutionalization at earlier vs. later ages, the type of institutionalization offered, experiences in the institution, and the perceptions of inmates at different ages, we believe that the difference in response between those who had been institutionalized vs. those whose cases were dismissed is sufficiently large that it would remain with these controls inserted. Again, there is no evidence that early institutionalization, i.e., severe sanctioning at an early age, was an effective deterrent to future serious offenses.

The Dynamics of Delinquent Behavior and Official Response

Table 6.3 helped us see why so much attention has been focused on the serious youthful offender. Although only ten persons with felony-level offenses were institutionalized at an early age, they produced none without police contacts and six with another referred felony within the next two years. The visibility of careers of this type gives rise to the idea of continuity in careers, interpreted by some as the failure of institutions to reform but by others as evidence of the consequences of early release. The problem is highlighted by the high proportion who only shortly after their early institutionalization returned to felony-level contacts that were serious enough to be referred.

Cohort members were examined, case by case, to determine if there was a link between discontinuity or complete desistance and institutionalization; in most cases where desistance could have followed, it did not. The reason or reasons behind cessation of contact-generating behavior would seem to arise from something other than time spent in an institution.[2] This does not imply that the explanation of continuity in careers vs. discontinuity lies within the person, in his/her psyche or immutable biological make-up.

Time lag between offense and imposition of sanction is often raised as a variable with the possibility of explanatory value. There was a lag time of one year beyond date of felony-level offense to sanction in 8.5% of the felony-level offenses that were sanctioned and 6.9% of them had a lag time of more than a year. Thus, in a few cases, the actual imposition of a sanction would be in a different two-year period than that in which the offense took place so that desistance based on the positive effects of incarceration, if it existed, would be found in the second or later following period. Other analyses of the Racine data have indicated that lag has little effect on outcomes for the Racine cohorts.

The ten institutionalized felony-level offenders, even if they were disproportionately referred for felony-level offenses in the next age period, made up only a small portion of those who had referred felonies in the next two-year age period, i.e., ten out of 139 persons who had referred felonies; in the next two-year period it was ten out of 132. While the institutionalized group had a greater probability of recidivism than others, the skewed marginals prevent the use of severity of sanctions as a predictor of future delinquent or criminal behavior. The results do indicate that greater use of institutionalization would probably have little effect on the overall delinquency and crime rate, i.e., would not reduce it. This has been said many times before, but not with longitudinal cohort data.

Effects of Demographic, Ecological, and Career Variables on Future Offense Seriousness

Having examined the data rather exhaustively with only controls for offense seriousness and disposition or severity of sanctions, our next approach was to determine if, as police contacts, dispositions, and sanctions accumulated, we could predict what would happen in the total future since next official offense is only an approximation of next actual behavior. Even if not much of the future is accounted for by the past, which parts of the past are most important, all other things being equal?

Thus, we turned to a regression model for the juvenile period (see Table 6.4) including the demographic and ecological variables, measures of present and prior career seriousness, severity of sanctions, as well as event frequencies. Only age at contact had statistical significance at each contact, first through the tenth; the younger the cohort member was at the time of the Nth contact, from 20% at the first contact to 39% at the higher contact levels the greater the proportion of the variance in future offense seriousness accounted for. In the adult analysis, age at contact was again the most powerful determinant of future offense seriousness, with prior offense seriousness next but significant only through the fifth contact. Although the analysis for the combined juvenile and adult periods accounted for up to 40% of the variance in future offense seriousness, only age at contact was statistically significant at all times, followed by race through the seventh contact and sex through the sixth contact.

These multiple regression analyses demonstrated that neither prior offenses nor prior sanctions had significant effects on future offense seriousness. While prior behavior and sanctions were significant in the first-order correlations, their impact declined when all other things were held constant. That race and sex remain tied to future offense seriousness is not a new finding. That number of sanctions had a negative impact on

TABLE 6.4 EFFECTS OF SELECTED VARIABLES ON FUTURE OFFENSE SERIOUSNESS AT FIRST TO TENTH OFFENSES; COMBINED COHORTS, JUVENILES AND ADULTS

Pearson Correlation for Contact Number

	1	2	3	4	5	6	7	8	9	10
Type Seriousness of Contact	.054*	.132*	.205*	.139*	.180*	.052	.133*	.162*	.111	.129*
Juvenile Neighborhood	-.183*	-.189*	-.185*	-.182*	-.182*	-.178*	-.183*	-.204*	-.192*	-.198*
Sex	.231*	.177*	.150*	.137*	.126*	.105*	.101	.094	.109	.118
White/Non-White	.242*	.232*	.221*	.209*	.203*	.211*	.197*	.188*	.170*	.176*
Age at Contact	-.409*	-.492*	-.537*	-.553*	-.562*	-.576*	-.581*	-.602*	-.599*	-.585*
Severity of Prior Sanctions	---	-.024	-.013	-.007	-.026	.012	-.042	.013	-.008	-.023
Total Prior Seriousness	---	.105*	.127*	.200*	.189*	.218*	.187*	.215*	.215*	.210*
Number of Prior Sanctions	---	-.100*	-.148*	-.122*	-.133*	-.141*	-.173*	-.165*	-.171*	-.152*
Severity, Present Sanction	-.048	-.008	.007	-.009	.038	-.045	.108*	.023	-.020	.028

Standardized Estimate

	1	2	3	4	5	6	7	8	9	10
Type Seriousness of Contact	.053*	.016	.054	.025	.066	-.024	.021	.042	.013	-.003
Juvenile Neighborhood	-.064*	-.065*	-.050	-.056	-.064	-.061	-.066	-.069	-.073	-.081
Sex	.147*	.098*	.075*	.078*	.086*	.088*	.067	.085	.092	.099
White/Non-White	.159*	.133*	.124*	.115*	.104*	.129*	.121*	.107	.108	.116
Age at Contact	-.337*	-.431*	-.471*	-.499*	-.508*	-.531*	-.533*	-.557*	-.564*	-.555*
Severity of Prior Sanctions	---	.010	.031	.025	-.008	.009	-.019	.018	-.020	-.062
Total Prior Seriousness	---	.029	.026	.038	.027	.071	.052	.051	.055	.054
Number of Prior Sanctions	---	-.048	-.070*	-.047	-.046	-.056	-.074	-.070	-.070	-.048
Severity, Present Sanction	-.022	.008	-.004	-.048	-.013	-.049	.031	-.016	-.076	-.008
N	2291	1608	1191	950	767	642	556	486	430	386
Adj. R	.224*	.278*	.320*	.331*	.345*	.369*	.372*	.395*	.394*	.373*

* Significant at .01 level.

(tended to reduce) future offense seriousness while severity of prior sanctions had a generally positive effect (tended to increase future offense seriousness) does not lend support to the position arguing for increasingly severe sanctions as the appropriate course to reduce future delinquent and criminal behavior. Furthermore, when variables were constructed which combined offense seriousness and severity of sanctions, there was no improvement in accounting for future offense seriousness.

Variation in Future Offense Seriousness by Cohort

The amount of variation in future offense seriousness accounted for by the regression model did not change drastically in the analysis when the cohort comparison was done for two of the three cohorts (1942 and 1949) as compared to the combined cohorts. However, a slightly larger amount of variation in future offense seriousness for the 1955 Cohort was accounted for by the model (ranging from 23% to 57% at the ninth contact) than when there was no control for cohort (22% to 39% at the ninth contact). Age at contact emerged as the most important variable in the regression model regardless of which cohort was under consideration, with coefficients that tended to increase from the 1942 Cohort to the 1949 Cohort to the 1955 Cohort. Overall, the other variables that had impact on future offense seriousness were race and juvenile neighborhood.

Accounting for Continuity vs. Discontinuity

While our explanation of future seriousness did not go far beyond what is generally accepted by other researchers, accounting for continuity or discontinuity has long been one of our concerns. With the dependent variable being continuity vs. discontinuity (desistance) from first through ninth contacts, age at contact was the only variable that was statistically significant from the first through the ninth police contacts for the juvenile and adult periods or without controls for period; the lower the age at any contact, the greater the probability of continuity beyond that contact. Age had its greatest effect during the juvenile period at the third contact, at which point 22.6% of the variance in juvenile continuity was accounted for and its greatest impact during the adult period at the first through fifth contacts, accounting for 11% of the variance. Without controls for juvenile or adult period, the second contact was the point at which the most continuity (22.7%) was accounted for. In essence, continuity vs. desistance was better accounted for than offense seriousness at any given police contact.

Even after the first contact more males had a second contact than di
not. The continuation rate was higher for males than females in the earl
stages of careers but they became more similar after the tenth conta
because a small proportion of the females were even more repetitious i
their behavior than the males. This is not true at the felony leve
however, where the desistance rate of females was high in every cohor
Those males who continued had more serious future careers than di
females who failed to desist.

Some Questions and Simplification of the Model

Before leaving the multiple regression analyses, there are sever.
additional questions that should be dealt with. Not all of the variable
were normally distributed, in fact, some were quite skewed. Consider
for example, those police contacts which were referred. Only 5.3% o
them resulted in institutionalization while 62.8% resulted in dismissal
The percent of referred contacts that culminated in institutionalizatio
varied from 3.7% for the 1942 Cohort to 5.7% for the 1955 Cohort. We
therefore, collapsed the categories for variables that were significantl
skewed and reran the multiple regression analysis, obtaining an Adjuste
R^2 of .359 at the fifth police contact compared to .345 with all variable
uncollapsed. Age at first contact had about the same weight as it ha
before collapsing (standardized estimate = -.497 vs. -598) and was th
only variable that had much impact on future offense seriousness. Se:
and race had almost identical standardized estimates as previously bu
seriousness of present offense became statistically significant with :
standardized estimate equal to that for the former. It was decided that the
skewed variables had had little effect on the outcome.

Repetition of the analysis with age at police contact and race omitted
resulted in no more than 9% to 15% of the variance being accounted for
Total prior offense seriousness and number of prior sanctions (cour
interventions) became the most important variables (the greater the
number of prior sanctions, the less serious the future career), followed by
inner city residence. In other words, the variables in which we were mos
interested, severity of present sanction, number of prior sanctions, and
severity of prior sanctions, accounted for only a small proportion of the
differences in total future offense seriousness, i.e., the seriousness o
future delinquent and criminal careers.

If *age at contact*, which may mean length of exposure to continue.
monitoring as much as an early start on a delinquent and/or crimina
career, and *race* are removed, prior offense seriousness, number of court
sanctions, and inner city residence become the only remaining variables

with statistical significance and these account for relatively little of the variance. It seems more and more that sanctions as administered during the period of this research had little or no effectiveness in specific deterrence.

Summary and Conclusions

Numerous analyses and reanalyses of the data, with cohorts separated and combined, with variables such as sex and race removed were conducted. Simply put, no evidence of deterrence based on severity of sanctions was found, although there was some indication that frequency of intervention was related to lower future offense seriousness.

One analysis after the other has by now suggested that structural variables were not only related to how juveniles and adults deported themselves but to how they were perceived by persons in the justice system. Social process theory goes beyond the explanations encompassed by structural theory and, as in the case of differential association, strain, control theory, etc., accounts even further for the development of delinquent attitudes and behavior. From this perspective we would, on theoretical grounds, hesitate to recommend increasing reliance on institutionalization as a sanction because it would seem to only further accelerate the acquisition of delinquent definitions and patterns of behavior. Actually, from both the structural theory and social process theory stances, placing a person in a delinquent or criminal subculture would maximize the chance of career development and continuity. Even if an institution went beyond warehousing its population and made a positive impact on its delinquent/criminal population, their return to the same position in the social structure, the same peers, and the same meaningful others would be most likely followed by a return to delinquency or crime.

Notes

1. *A More Precise Evaluation of the Effects of Sanctions* (Shannon, 1986b), National Institute of Justice Grant Number 84-IJ-CX-0013.
2. There were, as we previously indicated, 1,798 persons who had a police contact for non-traffic offenses during at least one of the two-year periods between ages 13 and 22. Among these were 119 who were institutionalized in one way or another as juveniles or young adults for one or more of these offenses. In addition, there were thirteen who were institutionalized (mostly jailed) for only traffic offenses (and seven who

received sentences of time in institutions for both traffic and non-traffi offenses). A check of the record of each of the 132 persons (all cohort combined) who had been institutionalized revealed that there were onl thirteen who had been removed from the community long enough to hav been unable to have contacts during the next two-year period(s).

If the other 119 had no contact it *could* have been becaus institutionalization was effective. Thus, failure to have additional contact because of removal from the community would account for only a smal proportion of the even short-time discontinuers.

Among those who ever received a sanction for a non-traffic offens were eighty-five who were in career continuity Type 5 (see Table 6.1) Of the total of forty Type 5 persons institutionalized, six received thei only institutionalization(s) at ages 21 and/or 22. Whether or not the were deterred in the following age period is not apparent from thi analysis. The remaining thirty-four were apparently undeterred, sinc they had police contacts at every age period.

There were 1,279 persons in the fifteen career types (Table 6.1) wh desisted after age 14, 16, 18, or 20, i.e., sometime during ages 1: through 22. They comprised 71.1% of the 1,798 persons with non-traffi contacts. Only fifty-one of these 1,279 persons in what might b characterized as "terminal career" categories had been institutionalized which is only 4.0% of those whose careers ceased before age 21. Eve if it could be assumed that institutional programs should receive the credi for desistance this would only be a small percent of the total number wh desisted for whatever reason.

Chapter 7

PREDICTION AND TYPOLOGY DEVELOPMENT

Introduction to the Offender Typologies

Our next project marked a return to the problem of predicting adult criminal behavior from juvenile delinquency.[1] This was combined with the development of offender typologies, following our contention that the problems of measurement, classification (typology development), and prediction are so intertwined that they require simultaneous consideration. Would combinations of police contact data representative of types of offense careers and combinations of data representative of the way the justice system had responded to them improve predictive efficiency over individual contact, referral, sanctioning, demographic, and ecological variables?

Developing offender typologies and testing their empirical validity was another step in the larger task of predicting adult careers from juvenile careers. Each type would represent a constellation of events rather than the sums of events.

We used the Gibbons typology (1965, 1975, 1982) as a starting point. Would these types or any other constructed types found in the literature (Chaiken and Chaiken, 1982) based on samples or populations of institutionalized offenders approximate our computer-generated types? Unfortunately, these typologies were not very useful in constructing career types from birth cohort police contact data because they consisted of categories for people at the serious end of the continuum of offenders. Only a small percent of a birth cohort is at the serious end of the continuum. Our task was to computer-construct a typology which would distribute cohort members over a fairly wide range of types but with the most serious defined so as to include sufficient members for statistical analysis.

Inherent in each type of delinquent career, it was hypothesized, would be a combination of events with a varied likelihood of producing continuity into adult crime. In pre-computer days the interrelations of variables making for continuity might be more or less impressionistically discerned but only by lengthy experience with delinquents and criminals.

Computer programs can cluster cohort members into relativel homogeneous types (the larger the number of types, the mor homogeneous is each), rank them in a way consistent with their conten and determine which type produced the largest proportion of continui into adult crime or the most serious of the adult criminal types, the latte also determined by computer.

This took us a long way from Shaw and Moore's (1931) model whic saw delinquent careers as gradually expanding from minor depredation to more serious index-level offenses leading to adult crime. It was als quite different from models of delinquency which concerned themselve with specialization, offender types as it were, such as vandals, shoplifters and, as adults, burglars and embezzlers.

It seemed reasonable that computer-constructed types would be mor efficient as predictors than additive scale scores, weighted or unweighted because they would represent meaningful clusters of offenses rather tha scores which could be obtained in a variety of ways but which did not tel us about the content of careers. They would probably not be specialize types of offenders but types in terms of what happens in the world o misbehavior. Furthermore, the juvenile types might be more closel linked to adult types than juvenile frequency and seriousness scores wer linked to adult frequency and seriousness scores.

Although there has been a vast literature on measurement, prediction classification, and typology development (Robison, 1936; Reiss, 1951 Meehl, 1954; Stott, 1960; Voss, 1963; Sellin and Wolfgang, 1964; Toby, 1965; Martin and Klein, 1965; Hirschi and Selvin, 1967; Blumstein anc Cohen, 1979; Monahan, 1978; Williams, 1980; Wilkins, 1980; Brennan, 1980; Monahan, 1981; Monahan, 1982; Rhodes, Tyson, Weekeley, Conly, and Powell, 1982), it has been almost uniformly disappointing There have also been several excellent assessments of the problem (Welford, 1967; Gottfredson, 1970; Chaiken and Chaiken, 1984). Mos recently, Gottfredson and Tonry's volume of edited papers (1987) cover the range of problems encountered in prediction and classification. In essence, anyone who attempts to increase predictability above chance o the modal categories of the marginals must realize at the outset that it wil be a difficult endeavor. Thus it is that prediction of what *individuals* wil do in the future does not come as easily as the prediction of wha *proportion of a group* will engage in delinquent or criminal behavior in the future.

Our first attempt to develop a computer typology was completely atheoretical. Data on offense seriousness, police response, and court sanctions by age period were subjected to the SAS FASTCLUS routine so that each person was placed in one of twenty-three different offender/justice system reaction types based on whether a person had had any police contact, if it was a non-traffic contact, a Part I contact, or a Felony-level contact, and whether that contact resulted in counselling and release, referral, or referrals and sanctions during each of three age periods (juvenile 6-17, young adult 18-20, and adult 21 and older). A person who had a contact that was both Part I and felony-level (this would also be considered a contact for any reason as well as a non-traffic contact) that was referred and sanctioned would be represented by four sets of three numbers each. The types which we are commencing to describe are shown in Table 7.1.

Each set of three numbers tells us whether or not a contact (the first number) occurred at each level of seriousness during each of the three age periods, whether or not the contact was referred (the second number), and then if there was a sanction imposed (the third number) according to a Yes-No at each incident. Logically, a No at the contact level must be followed by a No at the levels of referral and sanctions, etc. An 888 score tells us that the person(s) had a contact at that particular seriousness level in each age period (first number), a referral in each age period as a result of the contact (second number), and a sanction in each age period as a result of the referral (third number).

A person would be scored as all 8s if he/she had a Part I contact that was serious enough to be a felony which was referred and which resulted in a court (or agency) sanction during each of the three age periods. No one had this. Most who had very high scores, i.e., 8s and 7s, had many contacts in each age period, were referred each age period, were sanctioned each age period, but were not referred or sanctioned for a Part I or Felony-level contact during each age period. A person with an 8, 7, or 6 had more juvenile/adult continuity. Whether the continuity was serious or not depended on whether it was contact and sanction continuity or continuity in police contacts alone rather than continuity in sanctions. While some people may not find it difficult to have contact with the police, to be referred, and to receive a court sanction during each age period (particularly if well-known to the police early in life), it is not likely that many people will have a record of Felonies and Part I offenses with referrals and sanctions each age period.

One of the best attributes of this numerical representation of types is that it lends itself to easy translation into a description of the type of person or type of career that a person has had. It is easy to differentiate between people in continuous (time-spanning) trouble with the police and

TABLE 7.1 COMPOSITION OF DELINQUENCY/CRIME JUSTICE SYSTEM REACTIONS: CLUSTERS FOR COMBINED COHORTS

Cluster Number	Cluster Type[1] Cont	NonT	Part I	Fel	Mean Cont	Mean[2] Seri	% Felonies Prop	Pers	Tot[3]	% Part I[4]	% Male	Race/Ethnic W	B	C	Juv.Res. InnerC
20	888	887	777	777	38.7	3.4	27.8	8.3	36.1	30.0	100	44.9	49.0	6.1	67.4
8	884	873	773	771	22.4	3.4	23.9	11.0	34.9	28.3	90	47.4	42.1	10.5	47.4
15	877	877	555	555	27.1	3.1	20.6	7.7	28.3	23.2	96	62.8	29.4	7.8	45.1
22	555	555	555	555	17.2	3.2	26.9	6.2	33.1	28.8	89	77.8	11.1	11.1	33.3
7	551	551	111	551	4.9	3.4	14.4	16.5	30.9	7.2	50	90.0	10.0	---	10.0
17	833	733	331	331	9.3	3.2	18.7	11.0	29.7	41.7	81	61.9	35.7	2.4	45.2
4	511	511	511	511	4.3	3.2	25.5	3.1	28.6	28.0	71	76.7	18.8	4.5	33.0
18	551	551	551	551	8.7	3.2	20.6	6.1	26.7	23.5	85	74.4	21.3	4.3	40.4
11	855	855	111	555	9.9	3.3	8.9	17.7	26.6	9.6	75	87.5	12.5	---	25.0
21	875	855	551	551	23.0	3.1	18.5	5.8	24.3	17.7	85	73.1	19.2	7.7	46.2
14	885	885	421	311	3.1	2.8	6.0	6.7	12.7	4.4	60	86.9	5.8	7.3	21.7
16	551	551	551	111	4.2	3.1	27.7	1.0	28.7	28.6	62	78.2	14.5	7.3	27.5
6	873	761	551	111	11.4	3.0	16.1	6.0	22.1	17.6	61	76.3	13.2	10.5	39.5
2	855	555	555	111	11.4	3.0	17.2	3.9	21.1	18.8	83	69.0	10.3	20.7	51.7
19	851	811	511	111	10.1	3.0	14.0	5.4	19.3	15.4	91	76.8	19.6	3.6	35.7
1	871	851	511	111	14.7	2.8	13.1	3.9	17.0	12.1	81	80.7	16.1	3.2	32.3
10	875	855	111	111	13.1	2.7	3.1	3.2	6.3	3.3	71	81.4	10.0	8.6	31.4
12	851	751	111	111	5.5	2.6	1.8	3.3	5.1	.9	82	91.6	1.9	6.5	28.0
23	855	511	111	111	6.2	2.7	2.5	2.5	5.0	1.6	90	91.6	5.6	2.8	25.0
13	711	511	111	111	4.4	2.5	1.4	1.9	3.3	.9	70	89.9	6.7	3.4	22.6
9	511	511	111	111	2.0	2.6	1.5	1.8	3.3	.6	56	92.2	5.8	2.0	19.9
5	551	111	111	111	2.7	2.8	.8	.8	1.6	.8	73	95.6	4.4	---	16.2
3	111	111	111	111	1.1	.9	.3	.7	1.0	1.0	37	95.2	3.5	1.3	14.3
					[PEOPLE]		[% OFFENSES IN CLUSTER]				[CHARACTERISTICS OF PEOPLE]				

[1] As described on earlier pages.

[2] Offense seriousness: 6 - Felony against person, 5 - Felony against property, 4 - Major misdemeanor, 3 - Minor Misdemeanor, 2 - Status offense, 1 - Suspicion, investigation, information.

[3] This is also available by specific offenses.

[4] This is also available by specific offenses. For example, 8.6% of all police contacts by Cluster Type 20 persons were burglaries.

continuity in careers (except for Cluster 22). While a relatively hig proportion of the offenses in these clusters are felony-level and Part police contacts, several other types also have that characteristic. Perusal of the four cluster type columns in Table 7.1 enables the reade to see the variation in continuity for serious offenses, either felonies o Part Is, referrals for the same, and sanctions (if we think of cou appearances as part of the sanctioning process even though dismissal ma be the judicial action) from group to group. The next two columns shov the average number of police contacts and the average seriousness o police contacts by the persons in each cluster. The next three column indicate which proportion of the police contacts by each cluster's cohor members were felonies. The next column indicates which proportion wa Part I offenses. The next four columns show the demographi characteristics of cohort members in each cluster and the last column tell us the percent of each cluster's members who were socialized in the inne city.

The numbers representing Cluster 20, 888 887 777 777, mean that th typical offender in this cluster has probably been in almost continuou trouble as a juvenile, young adult, and adult, most of the time fo felony-level misbehavior and Part I offenses. We see that 100% of the forty-nine persons in this cluster are male, 50% are Black, 67% are from the inner city, and that the average person in the cluster had thirty-nine police contacts. The nineteen people in Cluster 8 are very much the same, not as many males, not as many offenses, not quite as Black, les than half inner city, and have been sanctioned less. If this typology system seems complex we suggest that the reader examine the contents o any issue of *Science.* the official publication of the American Associatior for the Advancement of Science. One should not expect behavioral type to be any less simple than the typologies utilized in the biologica sciences.

The second group, Clusters 7, 17, 4, 18, 11, 21, and 14, contains some clusters similar to those in the first group, although these cohort members have fewer police contacts. The third group's offenses are even less likely to be felonies, but some persons are included in these clusters who had felony offenses because they are most like these clusters in othe respects.

Cohort members who had relatively few offenses and these for less serious offenses, i.e., few felonies and few Part I offenses are in the fourth group. The last cluster, Cluster 3, contains few people who had had police contacts.

courts for minor offenses or non-offenses and persons who ha
involvement for major depredations.

Clustering the Number Sets to Produce Types

The data were subjected to computer clustering (SAS FASTCLU!
three cohorts combined and each cohort separately. The program
allowed to run for sufficient iterations to demonstrate that in-cl
homogeneity had reached its maximum without having too n
few-person clusters. This resulted in twenty-three clusters. In some c
the mean for a cluster, when rounded, was not one of the sixty-four ty
that are logically possible within each of the four offense/seriousness le
groupings (any police contact, non-traffic contact, etc.). In this case,
numbers were changed to the most frequent logical array of scores wit
the type.

The degree of homogeneity attained was sufficient that continuation
this approach seemed reasonable. The proof is in the pudding, so
speak, and it is a matter of seeing if being placed in a given cluste
identifies one as a meaningful type. There is, of course, always th
problem of outliers and a person may just barely meet the condition;
which place him or her in a number sequence or may go far beyond what
is necessary to fall into a sequence but still be lacking a justice system
reaction that would put the person in the next most serious sequence.
Thus, within each cluster there will be some outliers. The addition of
other qualifying variables may take care of the problem, as we shall see.

Composition of the Clusters

Having produced twenty-three clusters, what are they like? Does an
ordering of these clusters from the type perceived to be representative of
the most serious continuous delinquent and criminal behavior and judicial
system response to the least serious, i.e., non-offender type, result in
verification if we examine other indicators of career seriousness for the
cohort members within each cluster? Table 7.1 reveals that this approach
does a quite good job, better than any approach that we have yet
developed.

The various cluster types for the combined cohort members who had
had police contacts are arrayed in four groups according to their pattern
of police contact, referral, and sanction at various seriousness levels. The
top group includes four cluster types which to some extent distinguish
themselves from others (except for Cluster 2) by the number of police
contacts which their cohort members have had (Mean Contacts) and by the

The Distribution of Cohort Member
Differences by Cluster Type

Perhaps even more convincing of the heuristic value of this typology was the distribution of all cohort members across the cluster types according to their characteristics in a table (not included), arrayed in the same way as Table 7.1, all columns adding up to 100%. There were only 173 people in the first group of clusters, 4.3% of the 4,079 persons included in the analysis but 9.8% of those who resided in the inner city

Although the 173 people in the first group of cluster types made up only 4.3% of the total cohort, they were responsible for 56.5% of the property felonies, 58.4% of the Part I offenses, 78.2% of the burglaries, and 74.1% of the robberies. Although they were responsible for only 27.7% of all offenses, they are very serious offenders. These people, almost all males (but only .5% of the females and 7.4% of the males), have contributed disproportionately to the delinquency and crime scene and most have been known to the police and courts throughout much of their lives. They are more than twice as likely to be from the inner city as other cohort members and even more likely to be Black (17.9% of the Blacks are in this group but only 3% of the Whites).

Not all of the serious offenders are in these cluster types, but think again about Cluster 20, it has only 1.2% of the cohort members but 35.0% of the burglaries and 32.4% of the robberies. On the other hand, a high proportion of Cluster 7's offenses were felonies but none were burglaries or robberies. Ninety percent of the people in this cluster were White, it being the Whitest of the serious offender type clusters. These data underscore the problem in typology construction that Gibbons has talked about, the heterogeneity of people within some types in spite of some distinguishing characteristics which make the idea of a typology so compelling.

Each cohort was also submitted to the clustering routine separately to determine what proportion of the various offenses could be accounted for by a small percentage of each cohort. The eight most serious offender types in the 1942 Cohort contained only 5.1% of the cohort but each person in these clusters had had police contacts for felonies and Part I offenses. They accounted for 80.7% of all felonies by members of that cohort.

The 1949 Cohort produced seven types of felony/Part I offenders who constituted 4.5% of the cohort and accounted for 74.7% of their felonies. It took only four types making up 5.0% of the 1955 Cohort to account for 75.7% of its felonies. If three more types were added, all felonies and

Part I offenders, 7.4% of the 1955 Cohort accounted for 87.2% of i felonies.

A more detailed representation of the 1,279 members of 1949 Coho is found in Table 7.2. This approach enabled us to spoon out a high disproportional share of the serious offenders and, having identified them to focus attention upon them. For example (Table 7.2 for the 194 Cohort), although only 4.2% to 14.5% of the contacts for members c each cluster in the first group were for felonies against property, the accounted for 74.7% of all felonies against property, and 43.4% of thos against persons. They also accounted for 81.3% of the burglaries an 75.0% of the robberies. All persons in these types were mal (Table 7.2). Although they constituted 4.5% of the cohort, they wer 8.1% of the total males, were disproportionately Black, and/or wer socialized in the inner city. Looking at disproportionality differently these serious offenders (4.5% of the 1949 Cohort) included of 3.4% of th Whites, 10.4% of the Chicanos, and 18.0% of the Blacks. Perhap nothing is more intriguing than the results of a computer clusterin, approach which so effectively delineated a major share of the seriou street offenders. The typologies which we have been discussing however, covered total careers and it would have been difficult t disaggregate them to represent segments of careers and as juvenile, youn, adult, and adult for use in the prediction enterprise.

Other Approaches to Clustering

Our next step was to develop juvenile and adult typologies which migh enable us to increase our predictive efficiency over that obtained with th simple scoring systems previously utilized. Among other attempts t represent juvenile and adult careers were typologies based on numbe systems which not only took into account offense seriousness, referrals and sanctions, but also the relative frequency of events.

As in the first computer-generated set of clusters, each police contac by each cohort member appeared as a contact, whether or not it wa: referred, and whether or not it resulted in a sanction. The total numbe of contacts at each offense level and their disposition added up to a serie: of 2s, 1s, and 0s which represent whether or not the person was above o below the mean or had no contacts, referrals, or sanctions at each offens level. A series of 2s indicated that a person had more than the averag number of police contacts, more than the average number of referrals, an more than the average number of sanctions at each offense level (Felon Part I, Felony, Part I, Non-traffic, Traffic). A series of 2s would

TABLE 7.2 COMPOSITION OF DELINQUENCY/CRIME JUSTICE SYSTEM REACTIONS: CLUSTERS FOR 1949 COHORT

Cluster Number	Cluster Type[1] Cont	NonT	Part I	Fel	Mean Cont	Mean[2] Serl	% Felonies Prop	Pers	Tot[3]	Part I[4]	% Male	Race/Ethnic % W	B	C	Juv.Res. InnerC
11	887	887	877	775	37.6	2.7	9.9	2.7	12.6	22.1	100	71.4	28.4	---	57.1
20	755	755	551	551	27.6	2.8	14.5	2.2	16.7	24.8	100	80.0	20.0	---	40.0
13	888	888	655	655	53.0	2.5	6.6	.9	7.5	12.4	100	66.7	33.3	---	100.0
2	865	855	555	555	22.4	2.6	12.5	3.2	15.7	22.7	100	78.6	7.1	14.3	28.6
17	884	873	873	751	26.0	2.7	7.1	1.1	8.2	21.1	100	42.9	57.1	---	57.1
7	751	651	551	551	14.4	2.7	10.9	.9	11.8	17.9	100	75.0	18.6	6.2	43.3
21	887	877	777	333	24.0	2.7	4.2	2.1	6.3	18.7	100	50.0	50.0	---	25.0
9	851	651	511	551	9.9	2.7	7.9	4.5	12.4	6.7	67	100.0	---	---	11.1
14	888	885	421	311	32.3	2.5	1.3	1.3	2.6	6.6	86	85.7	14.3	---	28.6
6	873	873	551	111	16.9	2.5	4.3	.4	4.7	12.7	67	60.0	26.7	13.3	66.7
4	888	665	111	555	8.0	2.5	---	12.5	12.5	---	---	100.0	---	---	---
12	444	433	433	111	10.8	2.4	4.7	---	4.7	18.8	100	87.5	---	12.5	37.2
3	843	831	511	111	11.4	2.6	1.8	2.3	4.1	15.7	98	76.7	16.3	7.0	30.2
22	883	873	111	111	17.3	2.4	.2	1.7	1.9	1.3	89	81.5	7.4	11.1	33.3
18	511	511	511	111	4.5	2.7	3.3	.5	3.8	29.4	67	79.2	18.8	2.0	16.0
1	866	655	111	111	8.2	2.3	.9	---	1.8	2.9	85	76.9	7.7	15.4	30.8
19	851	811	111	111	6.3	2.1	.5	.8	1.3	.3	81	96.8	3.2	---	14.5
15	411	211	111	111	2.5	1.7	.6	.3	.9	.3	57	91.3	5.8	2.9	20.3
5	611	611	111	111	3.2	1.9	.2	---	.2	.8	63	91.1	7.4	1.5	21.1
8	551	111	111	111	3.0	2.2	---	---	---	.7	77	97.9	2.1	---	14.9
10	851	551	551	551	6.3	2.2	---	---	---	20.2	88	93.8	---	6.2	6.3
16	551	551	111	111	4.2	2.3	---	---	---	---	72	92.3	5.1	2.6	33.3
23	111	111	111	111	1.1	.7	.3	.6	.9	.5	38	96.2	3.0	.9	14.6
					[PEOPLE]				[% OFFENSES IN CLUSTER]			[CHARACTERISTICS OF PEOPLE]			

[1] As described on earlier pages.
[2] Offense seriousness: 6 – Felony against person, 5 – Felony against property, 4 – Major misdemeanor, 3 – Minor Misdemeanor, 2 – Status offense, 1 – Suspicion, investigation, information.
[3] This is also available by specific offenses.
[4] This is also available by specific offenses. For example, 11.2% of all police contacts by Cluster Type 20 persons were burglaries.

represent the most serious offender and most severely sanctioned type person with offenses, referrals, and sanctions at every level.

Table 7.3 is presented as an example of such an approach for tl juvenile period in which clusters are ranked from most serious to lea serious with sanctioning experiences taking precedence, followed t referrals and seriousness of contacts. In other words, how society hi reacted to a person's offenses is taken as an indicator of seriousness that career as well as the number and seriousness of alleged offenses. TI only person in Cluster 22 (Table 7.3), a unique person, was sanctione more often than average for offenses that were both Part I and felonie was sanctioned the average number of times for offenses that wei felonies alone, and received no sanctions for less serious offenses. Tl fourteen most serious juvenile clusters comprising 4.6% of the 194 Cohort population but 54.5% of its inner city residents accounted fi 72.9% of the property felonies, 62.1% of the felonies against person 48.5% of the Part I offenses, and even more of the burglaries (73.1% and robberies (81.9%).

Although there are many advantages to this clustering approacl Table 7.3 reveals there is little consistent variation in the characteristic of persons from cluster to cluster following the ranking of clusters i terms of their delinquent behavior patterns, the ages at which they ha their first police contacts, referrals, and sanctions at different offens levels. Furthermore, although persons in some serious career typ clusters are predominately from the inner city, others are not. Thi should not be surprising, however, because we have already indicated thi there was considerable heterogeneity within many neighborhoods, withi the inner city, but most of all in the non-inner city neighborhoods.

Some of the highlights of Table 7.3 are indicated by boxes. Note agai that cluster types representing high frequency of sanction, referral, an contact careers tend to include greater proportions of persons wit felony-level contacts, Part I contacts, inner city residents, and earlier ag of first contacts, referrals, and sanctions but that there is marke heterogeneity within every cluster. From the standpoint of prediction, thi the juvenile types did not correlate very highly with the adult types (.52 to .579), depending on the clustering system and cohort, was disappointment in terms of developing a prediction device.

Whatever value the typology has in terms of representing differer career patterns and delineating serious offender types, the problem o early identification remains. While the members of these clusters tende to find themselves in trouble earlier on the average by several years tha did others, differences between clusters are not clear-cut enough to b

TABLE 7.3 CLUSTER COMPOSITION OF JUSTICE SYSTEM REACTIONS TO DELINQUENCY: 1949 COHORT

Cluster Number	Cluster Type[1] Sanc 54321	Ref 54321	Cont 54321	Mean Cont	% Felonies Prop	Pers	Tot	% Part I	Juv Res % InnerC	First Cont	Average Age First Ref	First Sanc	First Fel Sanc
22	21000	12101	22122	19.0	36.8	---	36.8	31.6	---	14.0	15.0	15.0	15.0
6	20010	20210	20220	16.5	18.2	9.1	27.3	59.5	100.0	10.5	11.5	14.0	15.0
10	20000	20021	21221	32.0	15.6	.8	16.4	21.9	100.0	9.0	13.8	14.5	14.5
16	20000	10010	11220	15.0	13.3	8.9	22.2	37.8	31.1	11.0	13.0	14.3	14.3
2	10121	20222	20222	41.0	8.5	---	8.5	22.0	53.7	11.0	13.5	15.0	15.0
7	10100	21210	22220	21.5	23.3	---	23.3	62.8	53.5	9.0	11.0	12.0	15.0
9	10002	20002	20022	17.0	11.8	11.8	23.6	23.5	---	15.0	15.0	16.0	16.0
14	10000	12000	12100	50.0	50.0	25.0	75.0	50.0	100.0	14.0	16.0	16.0	16.0
21	10000	10020	10020	11.3	8.8	---	8.8	10.3	30.2	12.1	14.4	15.7	15.7
20	00020	00020	00120	8.1	3.1	---	3.1	10.9	61.5	11.4	14.8	16.1	---
1	00011	00012	00022	10.1	1.0	1.0	2.0	2.0	29.7	13.9	15.4	16.1	16.0
12	00000	20121	20121	8.3	27.3	3.0	30.3	36.4	66.7	13.0	14.5	---	---
13	00000	11121	11221	37.7	8.0	---	8.0	14.1	75.2	7.7	14.3	16.0	16.0
8	00000	10200	10220	12.4	9.7	---	9.7	35.5	72.6	11.6	15.4	16.0	---
23	00000	10000	10010	4.6	24.7	2.7	27.4	34.3	30.1	12.6	15.5	17.0	17.0
4	00000	00102	00112	7.9	1.4	---	1.4	31.0	45.1	12.6	15.1	16.0	---
19	00000	00011	00122	11.5	3.2	.8	4.0	12.2	17.7	11.8	15.2	16.3	16.0
5	00000	00010	00120	7.1	.7	---	.7	16.4	53.3	11.3	15.3	16.0	---
18	00000	00002	00012	4.0	---	---	---	---	8.8	14.0	15.8	16.6	---
17	00000	00001	00001	1.5	2.2	---	2.2	6.5	17.4	16.0	16.3	16.6	---
11	00000	00011	00011	3.2	.3	---	.3	5.5	16.3	13.1	16.0	17.0	---
3	00000	00000	00010	1.7	.8	.8	1.6	7.1	26.6	13.8	15.8	16.3	16.0
15	00000	00000	00001	1.1	2.4	1.2	3.6	39.0	4.9	15.2	14.8	16.0	---
24	00000	00000	00000	---	---	---	---	---	---	---	---	---	---

[PEOPLE] [% OFFENSES IN CLUSTER] [CHARACTERISTICS OF PEOPLE]

1 There are five offense types under contact, referral, and sanctions. Offense Type 1 — Traffic contact not felony or Part I; Offense Type 2 — Non-traffic contact not felony or Part I; Offense Type 3 — Part I contact not felony; Offense Type 4 — Felony contact not Part I; Offense Type 5 — Part I/Felony contact.

good predictors of serious delinquent and criminal careers, as careers ar
characterized and ranked by number of police contacts, referrals, o
sanctions at different levels of offense seriousness, with either offenses o
sanctions having priority.

In the next chapter we shall find where all of this has taken us, perhap
much further than we believe because each finding has led to another and
even if we do not have the "answer," we shall know why we do not ye
have the answer.

Note

1. *Prediction and Typology Development* (Shannon, 1987), Nationa
Institute of Justice Grant Number 85-IJ-CX-0019.

Chapter 8

TYPOLOGIES BASED ON OFFENSE SERIOUSNESS OR SEVERITY OF SANCTIONS

A Typology Based on Offense Seriousness

Our computer-generated typologies placed everyone in a cluster in a very straightforward manner, had an element of validity, as indicated by the heavy concentration of street offenders in a few clusters, but may be improved upon by other approaches which better represent delinquent and criminal careers and permit more efficient prediction.

The next typology, an example of such based on offenses alone, will be referred to as JCCARTY and ACCARTY. These types range from persons who had an extensive record of the most serious felony-level offenses to those who had few or no non-traffic police contacts in either the juvenile or the adult period. The development of this typology may be best understood by following our description of Table 8.1 for the 1955 Cohort.

Table 8.1 includes only three of the types (JCCARTY 1, 2 and 3). The entire panorama of types is shown for the 1955 Cohort in Table 8.2. The numbers from 1 to 24 were used as weights in determining each person's score (JCTOTAL). Perusal of the group whose members had one or more police contacts for robbery as juveniles reveals the heterogeneity of this group but also shows why they are considered to be all-around street offenders. The first person in this group has a score of 69 for robbery (23 X 3 robberies = 69) and a total score (JCTOTAL) of 202. The next person has a score of 133 under burglary (19 X 7 burglaries = 133) with a total score of 369.

The seriousness of each person's most serious offense determined the group into which he/she was placed.[1] Thus, there were armed robbers in the all-around street offender group (Table 8.1) who had committed numerous property offenses as well, followed by varied assaulters who had committed assault offenses but not robbery, and so on. There was also a group who were drug offenders and then a gaggle of burglars who also committed other property offenses. Note that the members of most groups were responsible for many types of offenses, particularly the first

TABLE 8.1 COHORT MEMBERS RANKED BY MOST SERIOUS JUVENILE OFFENSE IN CAREER SCORE: 1955 COHORT

		MISDEMEANOR LEVEL										FELONY LEVEL											

Column numbers: 1 2 3 4 5 8 9 10 11 12 13 14 15 16 17 18 19 20 21 22 23 24

JCCARTY — **JCTOTAL**

	1	2	3	4	5	8	9	10	11	12	13	14	15	16	17	18	19	20	21	22	23	24	Total
1	3	15	9					30		MURDERERS							57	40				24	179
2	3	12	18	4				40	11	26						19				69			202
	10	14	6	12				90		26		15		17	133					46			359
	2	14	21	12				70	11		28	60			19					46			303
	6	20	18					10												46			100
	4	6		4				10		13		15		18			21			23			114
	1		3									15			19	20				23			31
	2	14	6					110			28			17	18	24	7			23			465
	3	25	18					70				60		17	19	95				23			330
	5	19	6	16				40	11	52		30		18	76					23			295
	2	12	5	8				10		13	14	15			76					23			179
	1	5	6			8		30							57					23			131
	5	10	3					210						17	35	38				23			342
	9	25	9	8				70		13					36	33				23			232
	2	8	21						11	13				18	38					23			134
	3	6	3	4				50		26	70	75			33					23			293
	2	32	3	12				70							38					23			180
															38					23			61
	7	48	45		10			60		52				18	19					23			232
	1							20							19					23			53
	1		3					10							19					23			56
	7	14	33	4				20		104				18						23			223
	1	6	5	4				20						18						23			79
	3		15					10		13		15								23			79
	6	4	6	8				40		26										23			113
	2	5	4							13										23			48
	4							20												23			47
	3	4	5					10		ALL AROUND STREET OFFENDERS										23			46
			5					10		[ROBBERY MOST SERIOUS OFFENSE]										23			39
			3					10												23			36
				4																23			27
		4	9																	23			36
3	1	5	3	4						52								20	22				108
	4	14	33	12							105				76				22				266
	1	28	6	4		8		20		13		15			19				22				136
	3	8	6							13					19				22				71
	2	6						10		ASSAULTERS									22				40
	1	12	6							13									22				41
4	2	10				8		50	11	13									94				189
										SEX OFFENDERS													

group which we refer to as all-around street offenders. Although there is relatively little progression downward in total seriousness scores (JCTOTAL and ACTOTAL, right hand column of Tables 8.1 and 8.2), the average seriousness score of each type declines from type to type. The various juvenile types for the 1955 Cohort in Table 8.2 indicate that, even though we may characterize types in this way, many persons in the same serious types have usually had more offenses of less serious types than the offense by which he or she has been characterized. The literature has indicated that this *was* to be expected. Most of the 1955 Cohort members shown in Table 8.2 are males, few of the 1955 Cohort females were in any serious offender type as juveniles. Note that the all-around street offenders who had robbery as their most serious offense constitute a group that is not distinctly different (other than the robbery/burglary difference) from the lesser street offenders who had burglary as their most serious offense. At this point we shall say little about the felony drug offenders other than to note that their most consistent other offenses are theft. As a type, the variety of thieves is also apparent as a major grouping of types.

The same typology, applied to adults, places more emphasis on some types of careers than others in comparison with the juvenile period. Table 8.3 presents only the first panel of Table 8.4. It is in Table 8.4 where the importance of felony drug offenders is first apparent as a major segment of the adult offender types. Juvenile/adult differences are most easily seen by comparing Tables 8.2 and 8.4. Note that drug offenses are included as a part of the array of offenses for almost half of the all-around street offenders. Furthermore, drug offender types constitute (with the exception of traffic and disorderly conduct types) the largest group of adult offenders. Burglary, assault, theft, traffic offenses, and disorderly conduct are the most frequent other offenses. Similar tables are available for the 1942 and 1949 Cohorts but a detailed presentation of each would add little additional information, except to indicate that the drug offenders and drug offender types were almost totally absent in the 1942 and 1949 Cohort official records.

Although a variety of other typologies (offense typologies and sanctions typologies) enabled us to place cohort members in meaningful career types, none permitted an improvement in prediction of adult careers from juvenile careers beyond that obtained with simpler measures. Tables were also constructed which arrayed the 1955 Cohort members according to their juvenile and adult sanctions typologies, JPCARTY, APCARTY, JPTOTAL, and APTOTAL. These severity of sanctions types ranged from those who received no sanctions to those who had been

TABLE 8.2 COHORT MEMBERS RANKED BY MOST SERIOUS JUVENILE OFFENSE IN CAREER SCORE: 1955 COHORT

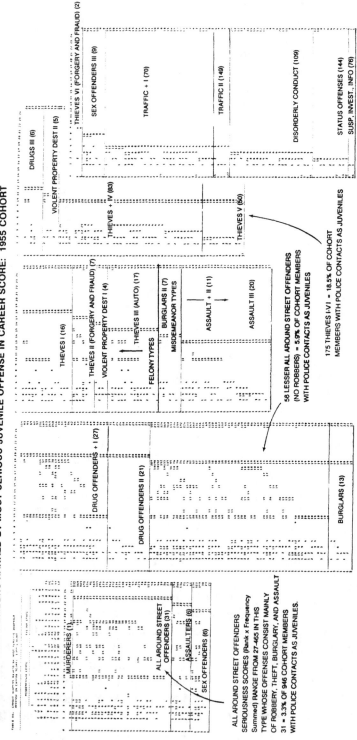

ALL AROUND STREET OFFENDERS
SERIOUSNESS SCORES (Rank x Frequency
Summed) RANGE FROM 27-465 IN THIS
TYPE WHOSE OFFENSES CONSIST MAINLY
OF ROBBERY, THEFT, BURGLARY, AND ASSAULT
31 = 3.3% OF 946 COHORT MEMBERS
WITH POLICE CONTACTS AS JUVENILES.

58 LESSER ALL AROUND STREET OFFENDERS
(NO ROBBERS) = 5.9% OF COHORT MEMBERS
WITH POLICE CONTACTS AS JUVENILES

175 THIEVES I-VI = 18.5% OF COHORT
MEMBERS WITH POLICE CONTACTS AS JUVENILES

MURDERERS (1)
ALL AROUND STREET OFFENDERS (31)
ASSAULTERS (6)
SEX OFFENDERS (6)

DRUG OFFENDERS + I (27)
DRUG OFFENDERS II (21)
BURGLARS (13)

THIEVES I (16)
THIEVES II (FORGERY AND FRAUD) (7)
VIOLENT PROPERTY DEST I (4)
THIEVES III (AUTO) (17)
FELONY TYPES
BURGLARS II (7)
MISDEMEANOR TYPES
ASSAULT + II (11)
ASSAULT III (20)

DRUGS III (6)
VIOLENT PROPERTY DEST II (5)
THIEVES VI (FORGERY AND FRAUD) (2)
SEX OFFENDERS III (9)
THIEVES + IV (83)
THIEVES V (50)
TRAFFIC + I (70)
TRAFFIC II (149)
DISORDERLY CONDUCT (109)
STATUS OFFENSES (144)
SUSP, INVEST., INFO (76)

TABLE 8.3 COHORT MEMBERS RANKED BY MOST SERIOUS ADULT OFFENSE IN CAREER SCORE: 1955 COHORT

	MISDEMEANOR LEVEL											FELONY LEVEL										

	C O N T A C T	D I S F C O N	T R A B I F L I N C	5 A M B I U F R G	L Q U O R	F O RF GR EA RU YO	T H E F T	D R O X	A S R A V U D S	T A AH UE TF OT	F O RF GR EA RU YO	T G H L F R R V P O	8 U R S O L A R G Y	A S U U R S S X	R S O B A U T	H O M B C I D E	TS OC TO AR LE
	JCCARTY																	
1	1	3	4	5	6	8	9	10	11	12 13	15 16	17 18	19 20 21	22	23 24		JCTOTAL
	15	4		8	10			15		36		161 24	273
	1 12	16			30 11	13		34 18	40		23 24	222
	1	8				13				22	24	68
	1 12	12				13	MURDERERS	20		24	82
2	3				10 11	15		76 40		161	316
	7	18		8	60	13			115	221
	1	60	5 5		10 11		57 20	22 69	261
	2 3	16	5	9	10		20	22 59	157
	4	5	8			57 20	69	163
	2		8			38 20	69	137
	1	30		20 33			44 46	174
	4	6			40	46	96
	8	8		20 21	23	80
			57	23	80
	6	8		19	23	56
		10	ALL AROUND STREET OFFENDERS	23	33
	1 3	8	[ROBBERY MOST SERIOUS OFFENSE]	23	35
	1	4		23	29
	6		23	29
	1		23	24
3	2	9	12	39		44	106
	3	15	40	22	80
	1	12	30		20	22	85
	2	6	12	6	10	57	22	115
	2	21	13	38	22	95
	33	10	26	19	22	110
	16	6	10	13	19	22	86
	2	24	4	13	22	70
	4	ASSAULTERS	22	26
	2	9	22	33
	9	22	31
4	3	18	8	19 20 21	89
	12	13	20 21	65
	1	12	18	21	52
	3 3	4	7	11	26	SEX OFFENDERS	21	77
	2	6	4	26	21	59

institutionalized for a year or more. Although these tables are n<
included, the sanctions variables will be described and utilized in some <
the analyses which follow.

The various typologies which arranged cohort members according t
their most frequent offenses or most serious offenses revealed that ther<
was considerable heterogeneity within types and that a large proportion o<
those who fell into the more serious types also had police contacts fo<
drug offenses. This is a finding to which we shall turn again becaus<
drug offenses may be the cement which links elements of some continuin;
careers.

Following the development of other juvenile and adult offens<
seriousness typologies and severity of sanctions typologies, we came bacl
to the question posed at the beginning of Chapter 7, will these type
permit an increase in predictive efficiency over that which had bee<
obtained with single measures of delinquency and criminal activity'
Maybe not. Even if they do not, a typology may yield other informatio<
of considerable importance, may shed light on issues that cannot b<
addressed with the measures that we have previously developed.

Comparing Measures and Typologies
of Delinquency and Crime

Our earlier juvenile and adult measures and recently constructed type<
are listed in Table 8.5. The first two measures, one of frequency o<
number of police contacts (JUVENILE and ADULT18) and the other o<
offense seriousness (JUVXN and EIGHTPXN), have been utilized i<
earlier analyses. The next three measures have not been previousl<
utilized in this volume but are fairly straightforward, weighted scores.
JCTOTAL, ACTOTAL (total offense seriousness from Tables 8.1-8.5)
JPTOTAL, APTOTAL (dispositions), and JPUNTOT and APUNTO<
(severity of sanctions scores) are similar types of measures.

The first of the typologies that were computer-generated, CLUS2RNK,
etc., was for total careers, while the second set of typologies are referre<
to as J2R1RANK, etc. These are followed by several sets of offense an<
sanctioning typologies, JCCARTY and ACCARTY (offender types),
JPCARTY and APCARTY (severity of sanctions types). JCEXRANK and
ACEXRANK are based on the types of police contacts or combinations o<
types of police contacts that made up 70% of a cohort member's polic<
contacts with the highest score being for those for whom 70% of his/he<
contacts were for offenses against persons. JSNEXRANK and
ASNEXRANK are based on types of sanctions that made up 70% of <

TABLE 8.4 COHORT MEMBERS RANKED BY MOST SERIOUS JUVENILE OFFENSE IN CAREER SCORE: 1955 COHORT

VIOLENT PROPERTY DEST. II (7)
THIEVES + IV (17)
THIEVES V (8)
VIOLENT PROPERTY DEST. I (4)
THIEVES VI (BURGLERY AND FRAUD) (9)
SEX OFFENDERS III (11)
LIQUOR + (14)
LIQUOR (11)
TRAFFIC + I (96)
TRAFFIC (317)
DISORDERLY CONDUCT (124)
SUSP. INVEST., AND INFOR. (56)

THIEVES I (14)
THIEVES II (FORGERY AND FRAUD) (8)
THIEVES III (AUTO) (10)
ASSAULTERS + II (6)
ASSAULTERS III (17)

78 DRUG OFFENDERS = 8.8% OF COHORT
MEMBERS WITH POLICE CONTACTS AS ADULTS

ALL AROUND STREET OFFENDERS (17)
[BURGLARY MOST SERIOUS OFFENSE]

57 THIEVES I-V = 6.6% OF COHORT
MEMBERS WITH POLICE CONTACTS AS ADULTS

DRUGS + I (34)
DRUGS II (42)
BURGLARS I (3)

MURDERERS (4)
ALL AROUND STREET OFFENDERS (17)
ASSAULTERS I (11)
SEX OFFENDERS (5)

ALL AROUND STREET OFFENDERS
SERIOUSNESS SCORES (Rank x Frequency
Summed) RANGE FROM 24-316. SEVERAL
COHORT MEMBERS WITH LOWEST SCORE IN THIS
GROUP HAVE NO OTHER ADULT OFFENSES
AND ARE OFFICIALLY ONLY ARMED ROBBERS
17 = 2.0% OF 863 COHORT MEMBERS
WITH POLICE CONTACTS AS ADULTS

TABLE 8.5 JUVENILE AND ADULT OFFENSE AND SANCTIONING MEASURES AND TYPOLOGIES

JUVENILE	Number of police contacts	6-17
ADULT18	Number of police contacts	18 +
JUVXN	Seriousness score: number of police contacts weighted	6-17
EIGHTPXN	at six levels from 1 for suspicion, investigation, or	18 +
	information to 6 for felony against the person	
JCTOTAL	Seriousness score: number of police contacts weighted	6-17
ACTOTAL	at 24 levels from 1 for suspicion, investigation, or	18 +
	information to 24 for homicide	
JPTOTAL	Disposition score: number of court dispositions	6-17
APTOTAL	weighted at 40 levels from 1 for dismissal to 40 for	18 +
	institutionalization of 1 year or more and other	
	sanctions	
JPUNTOT	Sanctioning score: same as JPTOTAL and APTOTAL but	6-17
APUNTOT	dismissals omitted from total	18 +
CLUS2RNK	Career type based on contact, referral, and	
CLUS9RNK	sanctioning for any police contacts, non-traffic	
CLUS5RNK	contacts, Part I contacts, and Felony contacts by	
	combinations of three age periods, 6-17, 18-20, and	
	21 + as represented by a series of 12 numbers from 1	
	to 8. This type represented total careers.	
J2R1RANK	Career type based on contact, referral, and	6-17
J9R1RANK	sanctioning frequency by offense type (Felony/Part I,	18 +
J5R1RANK	Felony, Part I, Non-traffic, and Traffic offenses)	
A2R1RANK	represented by three sets of five 2, 1, and 0 with	
A9R1RANK	priority to sanctions set in ranking	
A5R1RANK		
J2R2RANK	Same as above with priority to contact set in	6-17
J9R2RANK	ranking	18+
J5R2RANK		
A2R2RANK		
A9R2RANK		
A5R2RANK		
JCCARTY	Offense career type based on most serious offense	6-17
ACCARTY	in juvenile or adult period	18 +
JPCARTY	Sanctions experience type based on most serious	6-17
APCARTY	sanction in juvenile or adult period	18 +
JCEXRNK	Offense career type based on offense type or types	6-17
ACEXRNK	making up 70% of all contacts during period	18 +
JSNEXRNK	Sanctions experience type based on sanctions type	6-17
ASNEXRNK	making up 70% of all court dispositions	18 +

cohort member's sanctions. JNGHDUM and ANGHDUM were based on neighborhood of socialization and adult residence as inner city or other. The question is whether computer-constructed typologies represent careers better than do simple additive scores such as the number of offenses or referrals or the number of offenses of each type by their weighted seriousness. By better we mean that the typology permits better discrimination between inner city and other types of offenders and those with continuity vs. those without continuity than did simple additive measures.

Table 8.6 brings us back to issues that have been of major concern since the start of the project: (1) differences in findings based on the measure utilized or, as in this case, with the level of involvement which ranges from inclusion of all cohort members to inclusion of only those with sanctions and (2) the relationship between juvenile and adult misbehavior which, depending upon the measure utilized, may be just as much an artifact of justice system response as juvenile and adult misbehavior and continuity in misbehavior.

The first thing to note is that for all cohorts the juvenile/adult correlations are roughly similar for number of police contacts (JUVENILE/ADULT18), offense seriousness (JUVXN/EIGHTXN), and the offense seriousness typology measures (JCTOTAL/ACTOTAL). If only the level that includes all cohort members with or without police contacts is considered, the complex computer-generated typologies which took into consideration police dispositions, sanctions, and types of offenses (J2R1RANK/A2R2RANK, etc.) also produced similar juvenile/adult correlations.

Perhaps the most disconcerting aspect of the table is the irregular but consistent decline in the relationship of juvenile to adult careers as one proceeds from segments of the table based on all members of the cohort to only those who had been sanctioned. These lower correlations indicate that, in the end, there is very little relationship between juvenile and adult careers among those who had been sanctioned and, furthermore, that if there are two separate measures of members with sanctions, the measure or typology of juvenile and adult sanctions will generally have a lower correlation than will the measure of misbehavior.

The question becomes, how does an examination of the relationship between juvenile and adult measures and typologies help us improve prediction from juvenile to adult if the relationship between these periods is so low? Looking back, it seemed that even though the various typologies did not permit an increase in predictive efficiency between the juvenile and adult periods, they did tell us something about the complexity

TABLE 8.6 CORRELATIONS BETWEEN JUVENILE AND ADULT MEASURES AND TYPOLOGIES BY COHORT AND BY LEVEL OF JUSTICE SYSTEM INVOLVEMENT

	JUVENILE ADULT18	JUVXN EIGHTPXN	JCTOTAL ACTOTAL	JPUNTOT APUNTOT	JR2RANK AR2RANK	JR1RANK AR1RANK	JCCARTY ACCARTY	JPCARTY APCARTY	JCEXRNK ACEXRNK	JSNEXRNK ASNEXRNK	JNGHDUM ANGHDUM
All Members											
1942	.447	.456	.479	.388	.533	.549	.380	.335	.315	.347	.445
1949	.597	.576	.543	.274	.579	.569	.466	.366	.351	.396	.266
1955	.556	.562	.507	.323	.546	.526	.449	.380	.373	.397	.710
Members With Police Contacts											
1942	.377	.402	.427	.380	.364	.403	.250	.297	.238	.282	.393
1949	.558	.544	.512	.264	.436	.433	.349	.328	.280	.338	.267
1955	.502	.521	.472	.303	.361	.362	.311	.311	.287	.301	.632
Members with Referrals											
1942	.308	.326	.367	.362	.294	.308	.190	.242	.152	.199	.368
1949	.522	.498	.474	.238	.385	.336	.330	.266	.224	.258	.251
1955	.464	.474	.429	.263	.329	.201	.239	.203	.138	.159	.666
Members with Sanctions											
1942	.226	.251	.274	.282	.211	.075	.065	.082	.001	-.016	.490
1949	.456	.427	.403	.140	.278	.083	.322	.095	.169	.060	.218
1955	.452	.461	.413	.217	.354	.139	.324	.093	.292	.016	.706

DIAGRAM 8.1. JUVENILE OFFENSE SERIOUSNESS TYPE VS. ADULT OFFENSE SERIOUSNESS TYPE: 1955 COHORT

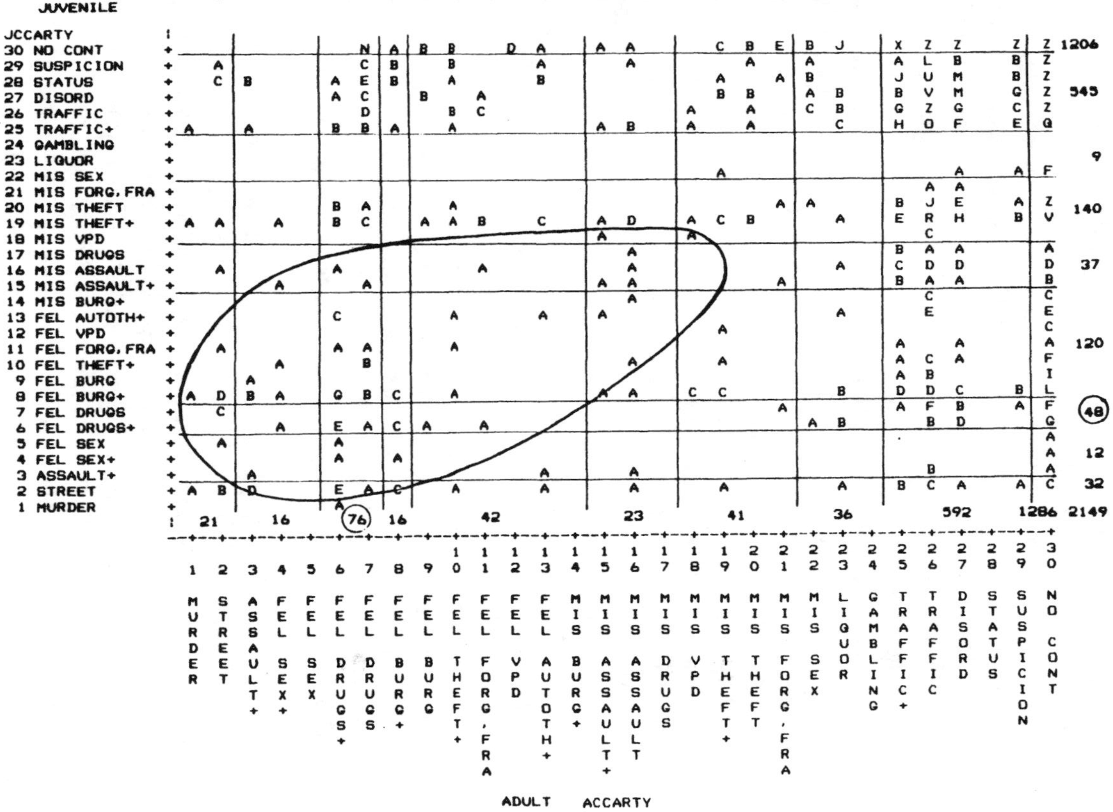
JUVENILE
JCCARTY
30 NO CONT
29 SUSPICION
28 STATUS
27 DISORD
26 TRAFFIC
25 TRAFFIC+
24 GAMBLING
23 LIQUOR
22 MIS SEX
21 MIS FORG. FRA
20 MIS THEFT
19 MIS THEFT+
18 MIS VPD
17 MIS DRUGS
16 MIS ASSAULT
15 MIS ASSAULT+
14 MIS BURG+
13 FEL AUTOTH+
12 FEL VPD
11 FEL FORG. FRA
10 FEL THEFT+
9 FEL BURG
8 FEL BURG+
7 FEL DRUGS
6 FEL DRUGS+
5 FEL SEX
4 FEL SEX+
3 ASSAULT+
2 STREET
1 MURDER
1206
545
9
140
37
120
48
12
32
2149
21
16
76
16
42
23
41
36
592
1286
1 MURDER
2 STREET
3 ASSAULT+
4 FEL SEX+
5 FEL SEX
6 FEL DRUGS+
7 FEL DRUGS
8 FEL BURG+
9 FEL BURG
10 FEL THEFT+
11 FEL FORG, FRA
12 FEL VPD
13 FEL AUTOTH+
14 MIS BURG+
15 MIS ASSAULT+
16 MIS ASSAULT
17 MIS DRUGS
18 MIS VPD
19 MIS THEFT+
20 MIS THEFT
21 MIS FORG, FRA
22 MIS SEX
23 LIQUOR
24 GAMBLING
25 TRAFFIC+
26 TRAFFIC
27 DISORD
28 STATUS
29 SUSPICION
30 NO CONT
ADULT ACCARTY

of the relationship between various careers (Diagram 8.1). They enable us to see which type of adult careers seemed to follow which type of juvenile careers. Typologies and scales were summary descriptive device that could represent careers even though they did not predict continuity We could say, for example, that 53% of the 1955 Cohort's juveni' all-around street offenders would, as adults, be in types ranging from all-around street offenders whose most serious offense would be arme robbery to lesser all-around street offenders whose most serious offens would be burglary. And, of those who were in these categories as adult only 42% had been there as juveniles.

How the data are arrayed depends to some extent on what we wish to do with them. In Diagram 8.1 it is obvious that felony-level career type as juveniles were in felony-level career types as adults more often tha were juvenile misdemeanor-level career type persons in felony-level adu types. A simple examination of the table showed, however, that no matte what juvenile careers were like, most had no adult offender career or wer in less serious offender types as adults. This is consistent with the hig rates of discontinuation found for both the Philadelphia and Racin cohorts.

The correlation between juvenile and adult career types was only .449 suggesting that the data were not of much use to persons on the firing lin in terms of predicting adult futures from prior juvenile types. Those who make decisions based on these data would be criticized for too many fals positives and too many false negatives were they to use juvenile career as predictors of adult careers. There are not enough reformatories o prisons to hold the false positives and there are too many critics o prediction to endure the serious misbehaviors as adults recorded by the false negatives.

Even if the offender types are rearranged so that felony types are immediately followed by their same non-felony types, there is littl improvement in predictive efficiency, i.e., false positives and false negatives remain large. When the self-report offense seriousness types for the 1942 and 1949 Cohorts were substituted for official types, there wa even less relationship between the juvenile and adult periods.

In the next chapter we shall discuss the nature of some of the continuity that did exist between types within several typologies and it is here tha we shall see how our data enable us to better understand the curren claims of a crucial relationship, an important nexus between drugs and crime. The question is whether or not it permits us to herald the battle against drugs as the best strategy in a war on crime.

Note

1. Our original six-point seriousness scale provided the first step in this expanded scale which arranged specific offenses within the felony and misdemeanor categories. Consideration was also given to Kathleen Anderson's report, "A Comparison of Two Offense Seriousness Scales," (Iowa City: Iowa Urban Community Research Center, 1984), 28 pp.

Chapter 9

DRUG OFFENDER TYPES AND THEIR RELATIONSHIP
TO THE ECOLOGY OF THE CITY

Introduction

Typology development set the stage for an investigation of how the behavioral content of some offender types when considered in their social context or societal setting might provide the cement for important delinquency/crime linkages or be the catalyst for continuity in delinquent or criminal careers.

This brought us to an analysis of drugs, delinquency, and crime based on the official and self-report data. These findings indicate that the distribution of types of juvenile and adult careers varies not only by inner city vs. other neighborhood residence but by whether or not respondents reported themselves as drug users (1942 and 1949 Cohorts) and whether or not cohort members had had a police contact for any drug offense(s) (1955 Cohort).[1] Let us look at some of the data but not jump to any hasty conclusions about how drug offenses are related to other kinds of misbehavior.

Offense Seriousness for Drug Users Compared to Non-Drug Users in the 1942 and 1949 Cohorts

Forty percent of *715 persons* in the 1942 and 1949 Cohorts who filled out self-reports and had continuous residence in Racine revealed at least some marijuana and/or other drug use. Police contact data for these self-reported drug users produced mean *official offense seriousness scores* of 11.8 for the juvenile period and 12.5 (only slightly less with drug contacts removed) for the adult period in comparison to non-drug user scores of 3.2 and 6.0 for these age periods.

The mean *self-report seriousness scores* for drug users of 45.0 for the juvenile periods and 60.1 for the adult period also contrasted with the non-drug user scores of 21.5 and 17.4. If self-reported drug use by the former was removed from their seriousness scores, their scores dropped to 43.5 and 42.0, still twice as large as the mean for non-drug users.

Of the 715 persons from the 1942 and 1949 Cohorts who submitte self-report forms, 353 had contacts with the police for offenses *other tha* traffic or suspicion, investigation, or information. The 54% of this grou who admitted drug use had mean *official seriousness scores* of 17.1 fc the juvenile period and 17.8 for the adult period (14.6 and 16.8 with dru offenses removed). The non-drug users (46%) had scores of 7.8 an 12.8. The mean *self-report seriousness scores* of this group were 52.(for the juvenile period and 66.4 for the adult period but dropped to 50. and 47.0 when drug use admissions were removed from their seriousnes scores. By comparison, the non-drug users had mean self-report score of 32.3 and 20.8.

No matter how we looked at it, self-reported drug users had mor serious juvenile and adult careers, official and self-reported, than did thos who did not report drug use. No causal statements are made, however because we have not yet dealt with the juxtaposition of drug and othe offenses. We are simply recognizing differences in careers that have als been found in numerous metropolitan areas and have been highl publicized in the media.

Offense Seriousness for Official Drug
Offenders in the 1955 Cohort

The police contact records of drug offenders in the 1955 Cohor produced *official seriousness scores* for the juvenile and adult periods o 64.6 and 50.1 (55.1 and 30.7 with drug offenses removed), compared to 8.2 and 4.6 for all of the non-drug offenders or 18.6 and 9.6 when the means were based on 1001, 1955 Cohort members with offenses other than traffic or suspicion, investigation, or information.

Offense Seriousness for Drug Offender
Types vs. Non-Drug Offender Types

No one argues that drug offenders/users, whether identified from official records or self-report, did not have higher total offense seriousness scores (police contact or self-report data) than did cohort members who were not drug offenders. *However, if the 1942 and 1949 Cohorts are dichotomized as drug user or non-drug user types on a basis of the self-report data, the official seriousness scores and the self-report seriousness scores differ less than they do when the dichotomy is based on official police contact data, i.e., had police contact for drugs or did not have police contact for drugs. In other words, those cohort members who admitted being drug users and whom we had placed in one of the drug* offender types on this basis, had, on the average, little or no more serious offense scores, official or self-reported, than did non-drug offender types, particularly if persons with only contacts for traffic or suspicion, investigation, or information were removed from the analysis. Moreover, *f offenses based on the drug use admissions are removed from the scores of the adult drug offender types, their mean offense score is lower than that for the non-drug offender types. Drug offender types are not always the most serious offenders overall.*

Some of the official record differences occur because the *officially* recognized/defined drug user/offender is probably not representative of all drug users/offenders. Many are lower SES and no matter whether engaged in crime at the moment or not are much more likely to have had and continue to have contact with the police than are middle and upper SES drug users who may be less active or not active in crime (Part I offenses). Where do lower SES drug users hang out in comparison with executives who purchase their drugs on the way home after a ghoulish day at the market? Anyone who frequents bars and taverns has seen and heard how these things happen in real life, even in non-metropolitan communities.

Comparing the Distribution of Official and Self-Report Types

Let us look at drug users vs. non-drug users in Table 9.1. The first set of percentaged columns under *Typology Constructed from Official Data* (Juvenile Drugs) adds to 100% for each column and shows that thirty-one respondents who admitted on the self-report that they had used marijuana or other drugs as juveniles were disproportionately classified as all-around street offenders, burglars plus, auto thieves plus, assaulters plus, thieves plus, and sex offenders, compared to those who did not admit juvenile drug use. It is not surprising that the 684 cohort members who did not admit drug use are far more frequently in the official No Contact category (58.2%) than are those who admitted drug use (25.8%).

The second set of columns (Adult Drugs) presents a different picture which must be considered because it suggests that 279 adults who admitted drug use do not differ from the 436 non-users quite so much and a greater proportion have not had their names in the police records. Perhaps this should not be so surprising because drug use during the period in which the 1942-1949 Cohorts reached the age of 18 was more commonplace than it had been during the period prior to their reaching the age of 18.

The third set of percentaged columns utilizes the *self-report offense typology*. Here we see that the thirty-one marijuana and other juvenile

TABLE 9.1 DISTRIBUTION OF OFFENDER TYPES BASED ON OFFICIAL AND SELF-REPORT DATA BY SELF-REPORT RESPONSES ON MARIJUANA AND OTHER DRUG QUESTIONS: 1942 AND 1949 COHORTS

| | Typology Constructed from Official Data | | | | | Typology Constructed from Self-Report Data | | | |
| | Juvenile Drugs | | Adult Drugs | | | Juvenile Drugs | | Adult Drugs | |
Types	Yes	No	Yes	No	Types	Yes	No	Yes	No
Murder	----	----	----	----	Robbery +	[16.1]	1.2	2.9	.9
Street	[3.2]	.4	1.1	----	Robbery	----	.1	----	----
Assault +	----	.3	1.1	.7	Weapons +	[29.0]	3.5	[13.6]	3.7
F Sex +	----	----	.4	----	Weapons	----	.1	----	.7
F Sex	----	----	.4	----	Auto Th +	[19.4]	6.4	2.2	.9
F Drugs +	----	----	1.1	----	Auto Th	----	.3	----	----
F Drugs	----	----	.4	----	Burglary +	3.2	7.7	3.2	.7
F Burglary +	[6.5]	1.3	----	----	Burglary	----	.3	----	.2
F Burglary	----	.3	.7	----	Steal +	----	2.5	.4	.2
F Theft +	----	.3	----	----	Steal	----	.3	----	----
F ForgFraud	----	----	1.4	.5	Assault +	9.7	16.7	[17.2]	6.9
F VPD	----	.1	----	.2	Assault	----	1.3	----	----
F Auto Th +	[6.5]	1.2	.7	----	Drugs +	3.2	----	19.0	----
M Burglary +	3.2	----	----	----	Drugs	----	----	.7	----
M Assault +	3.2	.1	.4	.5	VPD +	----	2.8	----	.7
M Assault	----	.3	1.4	----	Drunk D +	3.2	4.1	31.5	29.8
M Drugs	----	----	.4	----	Drunk D	----	----	----	7.6
M VPD	----	.1	----	.7	Theft +	6.5	11.8	.4	.7
M Theft +	[9.7]	5.6	2.2	1.6	Theft	----	1.9	----	.9
M Theft	[6.5]	2.2	----	.5	Marij +	9.7	----	7.9	----
M ForgFraud	----	.1	----	.2	Marij	----	----	1.1	----
M Sex	[3.2]	.4	2.2	.2	Liquor +	----	8.0	----	6.7
Liquor	----	----	2.2	.9	Liquor	----	5.7	----	5.0
Gambling	----	.1	----	----	Disord +	----	1.6	----	.7
Traffic +	12.9	5.6	10.8	6.0	Disord	----	2.5	----	.2
Traffic	12.9	11.0	24.8	31.4	Traffic +	----	.3	----	1.8
Disord	3.2	5.7	6.5	3.0	Traffic	----	.7	----	9.9
Status	3.2	2.6	----	----	Incorr	----	1.0	----	----
Suspicion	----	3.9	6.5	4.1	Contact	----	2.0	----	.7
No Contact	[25.8]	[58.2]	[33.7]	[49.5]	No Contact	----	17.0	----	21.1
N	31	684	279	436		31	684	279	436

drug users differ from the 684 non-drug users considerably more than they did when classified according to the typology based on official data. Almost two-thirds of them were included in the robbery plus, weapons plus, and auto theft type! The fourth set of columns is for the adults and, although the adult drug users do not differ from the non-drug users as much as they did among the juveniles, almost 40% were found in the more serious types.

Comparing Juvenile and Adult Offender Types with Control for Police Contacts for Drugs During Each Age Period

Table 9.2 utilizes the *official offense seriousness typology* presented in Table 9.1, applies it to the 1955 Cohort, and takes us a bit further in the analysis. It shows how the juvenile and adult distributions of cohort

TABLE 9.2 DISTRIBUTION OF 1955 COHORT: DICHOTOMIZED BY OFFICIAL RECORD FOR DRUG
OFFENSES DURING EACH AGE PERIOD

Police Contacts for Drug Offenses During:

	Juvenile Period					Adult Period			
Types Based	Yes		No			Yes		No	
on Official	Juv	Adlt	Juv	Adlt		Juv	Adlt	Juv	Adlt
Record	Typo	Typo	Typo	Typo		Typo	Typo	Typo	Typo
Murder	1.8	----	----	.2	Murder	1.1	2.2	----	.1
Street	1.8	5.3	1.4	.7	Street	11.2	7.9	1.0	.5
Assault +	1.8	----	.2	.5	Assault +	----	2.2	.3	.4
F Sex +	----	1.8	.1	.2	F Sex +	1.1	2.2	.1	.1
F Sex	----	----	.1	----	F Sex	2.2	----	-.1	----
F Drugs +	49.1	10.5	----	1.3	F Drugs +	7.9	37.1	1.0	----
F Drugs	35.1	1.8	----	2.0	F Drugs	2.2	48.3	.9	----
F Burglary +	----	5.3	2.7	.6	F Burglary +	12.4	----	2.2	.8
F Burglary	----	1.8	.6	.2	F Burglary	----	----	.6	.3
F Theft +	----	----	.8	.7	F Theft +	3.4	----	.6	.7
F ForgFraud	----	1.8	.3	.3	F ForgFraud	2.2	----	.2	.4
F VPD	----	----	.2	.2	F VPD	----	----	.2	.2
F Auto Th +	----	----	.8	.5	F Auto Th +	3.4	----	.7	.5
M Burglary +	----	----	.3	----	M Burglary +	----	----	.3	----
M Assault +	----	----	.5	.3	M Assault +	1.1	----	.5	.3
M Assault	----	3.5	1.0	.7	M Assault	1.1	----	.9	.8
M Drugs	10.5	----	----	----	M Drugs	----	----	.3	----
M VPD	----	----	.2	.3	M VPC	----	----	.2	.3
M Theft +	----	----	3.9	.8	M Theft +	5.6	----	3.7	.8
M Theft	----	----	2.4	.4	M Theft	3.4	----	2.3	.4
M ForgFraud	----	1.8	.1	.4	M ForgFraud	----	----	.1	.4
M Sex	----	1.8	.4	.5	M Sex	----	----	.4	.5
Liquor	----	5.3	----	1.1	Liquor	----	----	----	1.2
Gambling	----	----	----	----	Gambling	----	----	----	----
Traffic +	----	5.3	3.2	3.5	Traffic +	5.6	----	3.0	3.7
Traffic	----	15.8	7.3	15.6	Traffic	4.5	----	7.2	16.3
Disord	----	12.3	5.2	5.6	Disord	4.5	----	5.1	6.0
Status	----	----	6.9	----	Status	7.9	----	6.7	----
Suspicion	----	1.8	3.5	2.6	Suspicion	3.4	----	3.4	2.7
No Contact	----	24.6	57.6	60.8	No Contact	15.1	----	57.8	62.4
N	57	57	2092	2092	N	89	89	2060	2060
In Traffic or Less Serious	59.8	83.7	88.1					83.2	91.1

members by offense types vary by whether or not 1955 Cohort members had had police contacts for drug offenses as juveniles or adults.

The distribution of offense types in the first set of columns reveals that 84.2% fell in drug offender types as juveniles but only 12.3% did so as adults. Most of those fifty-seven who had police contacts for drug offenses as juveniles and who were classified as juvenile drug-offender types based on their pattern of juvenile police contacts must, as adults, have had relatively less drug activity, not have had police contacts for their drug activity, or were, in a few cases, in a more serious offender type. By contrast, there were relatively few cohort members in the serious offender types as either juveniles or adults among those 2,092,

1955 Cohort members who had not had police contacts for drugs as juveniles.

The distribution of offender types in the adult period indicates that mo of that 85.4% of the adults in the drug offender types, among thos eighty-nine who had police contacts for drugs as adults, had not bee involved in drugs as juveniles, had not had their involvement detected b the police, or had been placed in more serious offense categories (becaus they had some offenses that were more serious than drugs).

Those who had not had police contacts for drug offenses as adult appear to have had relatively little serious misbehavior as either juvenile or adults. These data do not, however, provide a basis for claims of causal nexus between drugs, delinquency, and crime or the developmen of criminal types as a consequence of drug use.

The Relationship of Juvenile Offender Types to Adult Offender Types: Drug Offenders vs. Non-Drug Offenders

Diagram 9.1 is based on the official offense seriousness typology use in Tables 9.1 and 9.2. This diagram shows the typological distribution o the 136, 1955 Cohort members who had police contacts for drug offenses About 60% of the cohort's most serious juvenile offender types and 45% of its most serious adult offender types are included in Diagram 9.1. The 2,013 cohort members not included in this diagram constituted the othe 94.5% of the cohort. There were only twenty-one serious continuit types, about 1% of the group in comparison with 35.3% of these who ha had police contacts for drug offenses. In neither group was there a really straightforward relationship between police contact patterns or types as a juvenile and police contact patterns or types as an adult. If both of the groups were placed together, the correlation between juvenile and adul offense seriousness types would be .449.

There were more persons observed than expected in the lower left hand corner of Diagram 9.1, i.e., the very bad tended to remain bac disproportionately to those who were in serious offender types as adult (although some changed for the better). While there were forty-eigh persons in the felony-level drug types as juveniles, most of them did no appear in felony drug types as adults. Most of the seventy-six in felony drug types as adults had not been in the juvenile felony-level drug type but thirty-one had been in various other felony types. Only fourteen o the seventy-six had not had a police contact as a juvenile. What would interviews tell us about how the forty-four new adult felony drug offende types differ from the thirty-three who were drug offender types as juveniles who had desisted from serious crime as adults? All of this tends

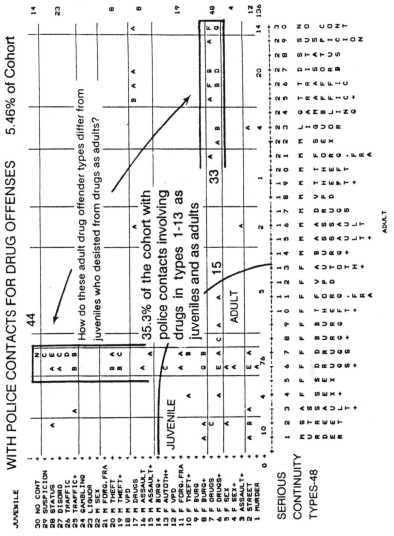

DIAGRAM 9.1 JUVENILE OFFENSE SERIOUSNESS TYPE VS. ADULT OFFENSE SERIOUSNESS TYPE: PERSONS IN 1955 COHORT

125

WITH POLICE CONTACTS FOR DRUG OFFENSES   5.46% of Cohort

How do these adult drug offender types differ from juveniles who desisted from drugs as adults?

35.3% of the cohort with police contacts involving drugs in types 1-13 as juveniles and as adults to upset those who are sure that early drug use is a precursor to seriou criminal careers or that adult drug offender types may be readily predicte by their juvenile behavior. That there is a delinquency/drug/crime nexu we can be sure but that it is not a simple relationship we can also b sure. How it is compounded by the police and court policy is anothe matter which cannot be discerned by the content of official records alone

The Relationship of Juvenile Types to Adult Types:
Self-Report Data

Since official records seem to under-report drug offenses more tha many other offenses, we now turn back to the 1942 and 1949 Cohort where we had fewer official drug contacts but *self-report* data tha included the use of marijuana, the use of other drugs, and two categorie on alcohol use.

The typology based on the self-report data is similar but not identica to that based on official data. It varies because there were som differences in the offense categories utilized and because the *officia offense seriousness* typology was based on the number of offenses i official records while the *self-report typology* was based on what peopl were willing to report about themselves in categories: (1) once or twic (very rarely), (2) occasionally, (3) frequently, and (4) all the time.

Table 9.3 (adult types as an example) indicates how marijuana anc other drug offenses are included in a variety of offense types commencin with robbery plus, the all-around street offender type, at the adult level What we wish to show is the extent to which self-reported drugs, at leas marijuana, are found throughout the various types. As we have indicated persons with felony-level drug offenses were found in the more seriou types but, unless these drug offenses were committed prior to and led t other offenses, knowledge of drug offenses would be of little help i predicting serious criminal careers. We shall deal with that question a bi later.

When Diagram 9.2 (similar to Diagram 8.1 in Chapter 8) wa constructed based on the *self-report typology*, the most serious types o juveniles were found in the most serious types as adults to only a limitec extent, although in some cells quite disproportionately to the number tha would be expected based on a chance number computed from th marginals. These are the same data as shown in the self-report typolog columns of Table 9.1 in this chapter as percentages for juveniles anc adults but letters represent the numbers in each cell in Diagram 9.2 A = 1, B = 2, etc., to Z, which = 26 or + cohort members.

TABLE 9.3 COHORT MEMBERS RANKED BY MOST SERIOUS ADULT SELF-REPORT OFFENSE: 1942 AND 1949 COHORTS

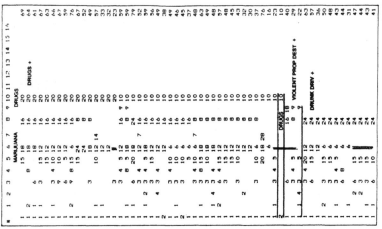

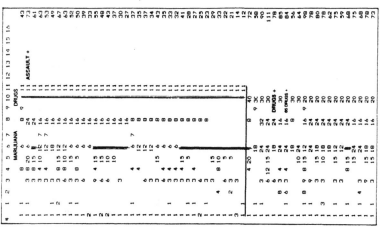

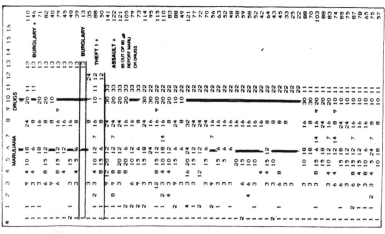

(continued)

129

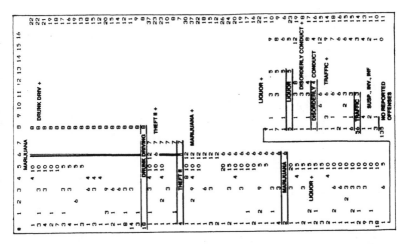

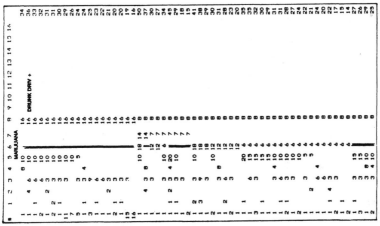

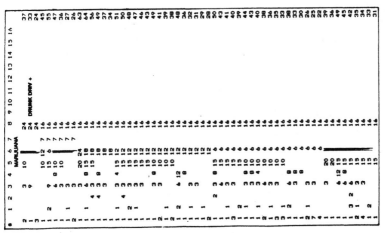

DIAGRAM 9.2. JUVENILE SELF-REPORT OFFENSE SERIOUSNESS TYPE VS ADULT SELF-REPORT OFFENSE SERIOUSNESS TYPE: 1942-1949 COHORT

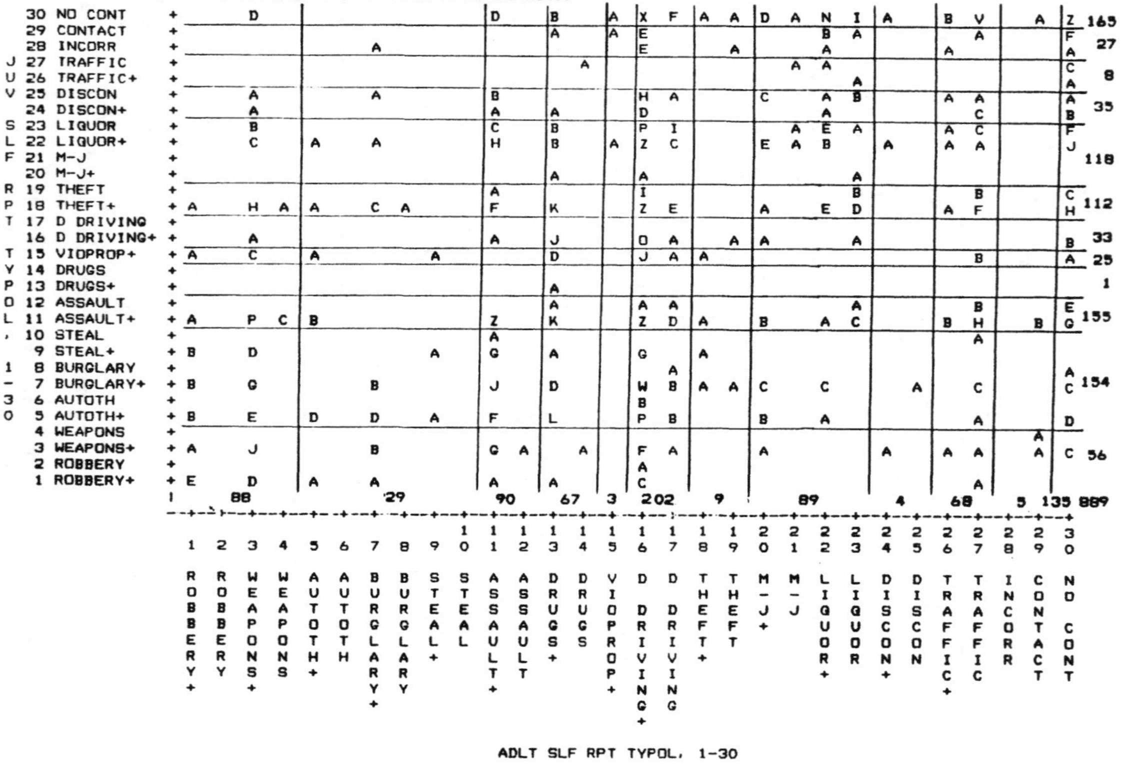

		Z	
30	NO CONT	A	165
29	CONTACT	F	27
28	INCORR	C	8
27	TRAFFIC	A	35
26	TRAFFIC+	B	
25	DISCDN	F	118
24	DISCDN+	J	
23	LIQUOR		
22	LIQUOR+	C / H	112
21	M-J		
20	M-J+	B	33
19	THEFT	A	25
18	THEFT+		1
17	D DRIVING	E	155
16	D DRIVING+	G	
15	VIOPROP+	A / C	154
14	DRUGS		
13	DRUGS+	D	56
12	ASSAULT	C	
11	ASSAULT+		
10	STEAL		
9	STEAL+		
8	BURGLARY		
7	BURGLARY+		
6	AUTOTH		
5	AUTOTH+		
4	WEAPONS		
3	WEAPONS+		
2	ROBBERY		
1	ROBBERY+		

ADLT SLF RPT TYPOL. 1-30

Most noticeable was the relationship between: (1) juvenile thieves and adult assaulters, weapons offenders and drug offenders and drunk drivers (driving under the influence of alcohol or drugs), (2) juvenile assaulters and adult assaulters, weapons offenders, drug offenders, and drunk drivers, (3) juvenile burglars and adult weapons offenders, assaulters, and drunk drivers, and (4) a range of other lesser juvenile offenses and adult drunk drivers. Continuity was, in fact, not from offense type to similar offense type, as much as from a whole variety of interrelated serious and not serious juvenile offense types to adult weapons offenders, assaulters, drug offenders, and *drunk driving plus other lesser offenses included* in each adult type. There was also considerable desistance from the most serious to less serious offender types. Although several juvenile types led to adult drug types, even more juvenile offense types led to adult driving under the influence.

Before the reader concludes that some kind of causal tie has appeared, it should be noted that the marginal totals for offense types markedly changed between the juvenile and adult periods. Only thirty-three juveniles reported their behavior in such a way as to fall into the drunk driving (driving under the influence) type but 202 did so as adults.

A wide variety of behaviors reported during the teens tapered off so that as adults these juveniles were now in the driving under the influence category, a more or less natural transition as driving licenses were obtained and automobiles became available. Concomitant with this was the increase in traffic offenders from eight to sixty-eight. All of this, of course, suggests greater patterned continuity than had been found from analysis of the official police records.

To make the point, we dichotomized the 1942 and 1949 Cohort members with continuous residence (715) into those 286 who had *self-reported* drug use for Diagram 9.3A and those 429 who had not for Diagram 9.3B. This was the 40%-60% division mentioned earlier. Diagram 9.3B dramatizes how 96% of the non-drug users were concentrated in the upper right hand corner in the least serious police contact offender types as juveniles and adults. This utilized the same typology based on police contact data (offense record typology) that was used in Diagram 9.1. Diagram 9.3A reveals that marijuana and other drug users, although 86% of them were concentrated in the upper right hand corner of the diagrams, were also found in some of the most serious types as juveniles and/or adults. Serious offense continuity was considerably more evident among those who had reported themselves as drug user/offenders.

132

DIAGRAM 9.3 JUVENILE OFFENSE SERIOUSNESS TYPE VS. ADULT OFFENSE SERIOUSNESS TYPE: 1942-1949 COHORTS

A. MEMBERS REPORTING DRUG USE   40.0% of Cohort   86% of the Cohort reporting drug use in types 18-30 juvenile & adult.

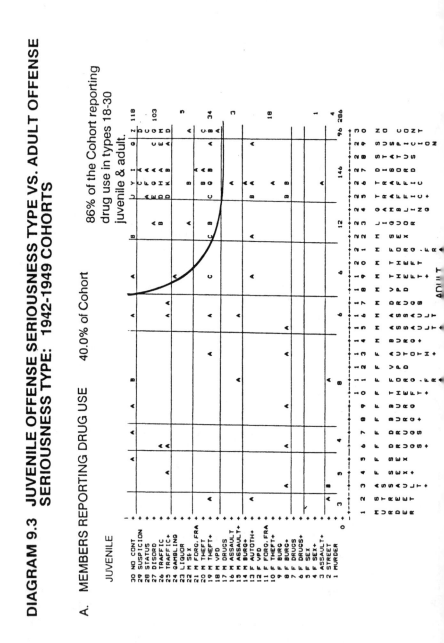

133

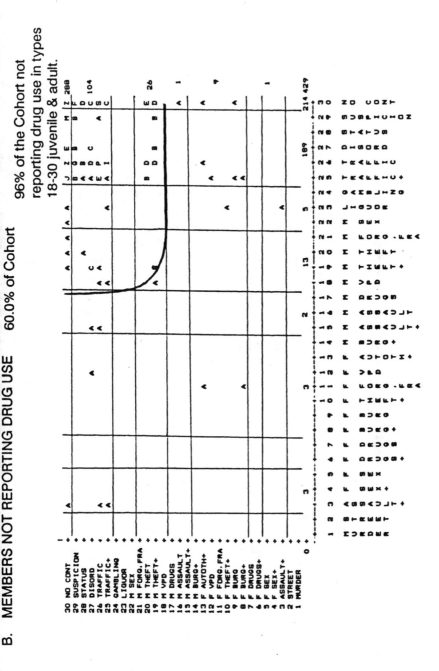

B. MEMBERS NOT REPORTING DRUG USE   60.0% of Cohort

96% of the Cohort not reporting drug use in types 18-30 juvenile & adult.

This still does not tell us that marijuana and drug use led ♦ delinquency and crime or to continuities in either during the 195(through the early 1970s because most of the 1942 and 1949 Coho members, drug users or not, had rather modest careers in delinquency an crime. *The question remains, why were some of the drug users als serious delinquents and/or criminals?*

The Ecology of Drugs and Serious Crime

Racine's sixty-five relatively homogeneous neighborhoods were arraye within four major categories, inner city, transitional, stable, an peripheral, according to the proportion of the all-around street offender found in each neighborhood. Much of the delinquency and crime i concentrated in only ten inner city and transitional neighborhoods. Seve of these inner city neighborhoods had disproportional shares of th all-around street offenders. Neighborhood 11, for example, containe only 1.4% of Racine's population but contained 8.4% of those 195 Cohort members who were in the all-around street offender type a juveniles and 12.5% in that type as adults. Few neighborhoods had a sizeable a proportion of the persons who were drug offenders as juvenile and adults as did inner city Neighborhoods 11 and 5.

The distribution of self-reported drug users, juvenile or adult, wa fairly congruent with the distribution for those who filled out th self-report forms that were presented to them at the time of the interview A portion of the difference between self-reported drug use/offenses an official records of contacts for drug offenses may be attributed to ; difference in patterns of drug use and trafficking. The former is mor widespread and the latter, followed by law enforcement, has a patter which is not congruent with simple drug use.

Table 9.4 presents data on nineteen of the sixty-five neighborhoods officially the most troublesome types of neighborhoods. While onl 20.6% of the 1955 Cohort resided in the ten neighborhoods from the inne city and transitional areas as juveniles, 55.2% of the juvenile all-aroun street offenders resided in these neighborhoods and 67.2% of those wh were street offenders as adults also resided there as juveniles. In contras only 19.0% as juveniles and 39.0% as adults of the cohort members wit drug offenses were from these neighborhoods. What does this do to th drugs cause crime, the crime causes drugs, or the common caus explanations of the drug/crime link?

Since we do not have self-report data on the 1955 Cohort, we turne back to the 1942 and 1949 Cohorts and found that 20.3% of those wh admitted drug use as juveniles and 19.6% who did so as adults were from

TABLE 9.4   ALL-AROUND STREET OFFENDERS, DRUG OFFENDERS, AND SELF-REPORTED DRUG OFFENDERS

% 1955 Cohort in NGH	Police Contacts % All-Around Street Offenders in Neighborhoods		Police Contacts % Drug Offenders in Neighborhoods		Self Report % 1942/49 Cohorts in Ngs.	Self-Report % Reporting Drug Offenses in NGSs	
	Juv.	Adult	Juv.	Adult		Juv.	Adult
7 Inner City							
15.6	45.6	50.0	9.5	(33.0)	15.7	15.1	14.8
3 Interstitial or Transitional							
5.0	9.6	18.9	9.5	6.0	5.1	5.2	4.8
20.6	55.2	68.9	19.0	39.0	20.8	20.3	19.6
5 Stable							
11.5	3.6	6.2	9.5	6.0	14.4	13.1	18.4
4 Peripheral							
7.8	2.4	3.1	17.3	12.0	4.6	4.8	5.2
19.3	6.0	9.3	26.8	18.0	19.0	17.9	23.6
Total							
39.9	61.2	78.2	45.8	57.0	39.8	38.2	43.2

these neighborhoods, proportions similar to the proportion of self-reports (20.8%) obtained from these neighborhoods. In other words, self-reported drug offenders were not distributed in neighborhoods disproportionately to their numbers in the 1942 and 1949 Cohorts.

The widespread prevalence of drug use was further demonstrated when we turned to the nine Stable and Peripheral neighborhoods which produced about the same proportion of self-reported drug offenders (17.9% and 23.6%) and contained the same proportion of the population as did the ten inner city and interstitial neighborhoods. These neighborhoods produced a relatively small proportion of the all-around street offenders (6.0% and 9.3%) but 26.8% of the drug offenders who had their first offense as juveniles and 18.5% of those who had their first drug contact after the age of 18. Thus, it would seem, there are drug offenders whose offenses are part of a larger offense career, those whose drug offenses probably have little to do with either delinquency or crime, and those whose delinquency and crime have little to do with drugs. We have suggested this before but had not arranged the data in this fashion.

Continuity in Careers: Inner City vs. Other Neighborhoods and Drug Users/Offenders vs. Non-Users/Non-Offenders

Since we have referred to the continuity in careers between the juvenile and adult periods, the question arose as to where the continuity was greatest for drug users/offenders vs. non-users/non-offenders. We have produced a dozen tables which shed some light on this question. Everyone in the 1942 and 1949 Cohorts was dichotomized as self-reported drug user/non-user because there were too few who had drug offenses on their records to include a dichotomy based on official records. Both of the career typologies, self-reported and official, were utilized.

When the *self-report typology* was considered, the relationship of juvenile to adult careers was greater among inner city non-drug user (.4757) than among drug users (.3447), less in each case among those who resided in non-inner city neighborhoods as juveniles. Simple self-report seriousness scores between the juvenile and adult periods were correlated even higher for the same dichotomies (drug users .7512 and

TABLE 9.5   RELATIONSHIP OF JUVENILE TYPES AND TOTAL OFFENSE SERIOUSNESS TO ADULT TYPES AND TOTAL OFFENSE SERIOUSENSS WITH CONTROLS FOR DRUG USER/ OFFENDER VS. NON-DRUG USER/OFFENDER AND PLACE OF JUVENILE RESIDENCE*

1 9 4 2 - 1 9 4 9   C o h o r t s

	Self-Report Typology		Self-Report Seriousness Scores	
	Drug Users	Non-Users	Drug Users	Non-Users
Inner City	.3447	.4757	.7512	.7253
Non-Inner City	.1995	.3234	.4535	.4065

	Official Offense Seriousness Typology		Official Offense Seriousness Scores	
	Drug Users	Non-Users	Drug Users	Non-Users
Inner City	.6775	.5292	.7828	.6262
Non-Inner City	.3375	.1163 ns	.4405	.1832

1 9 5 5   C o h o r t

	Official Offense Seriousness Typology		Official Offense Seriousness Scores	
	Drug Offenders	Non-Offenders	Drug Offenders	Non-Offenders
Inner City	-.1177 ns	.3941	.4807	.4213
Non-Inner City	-.4514	.3654	.3710	.3520

* Pearsonian Correlation Coefficients significant at .01 level or greater unless indicated.

non-users .7523). What this indicates, as shown in Table 9.5, is that seriousness had more continuity than did specific types of offenses and, as we have so often stated, continuity was higher in the inner city than in other neighborhoods.

When the *official typology* was used in place of the self-report typology (next lower panel of Table 9.5) data for the 1942 and 1949 Cohorts, the correlation indicating career continuity was highest (.6755) for inner city drug users, next for non-drug users (.5292). Official offense seriousness scores produced even greater evidence of higher inner city continuity for drug users (.7828) but also considerable continuity for non-users (.6262). What we must realize is that in the segments of Table 9.5 which we have just described, each divided into four groups by the drug use/non-use and inner city/non-inner city dichotomies, most of the continuity, with the exception of the self-report typology, is based on the continuity of offenses other than drug offenses because there were very few police contacts for drug offenses during either entire period of the 1942 and 1949 Cohorts.

When the 1955 Cohort was dichotomized (utilizing police contact records) as drug offenders vs. non-drug offenders and inner city vs. other juvenile place of residence, it was apparent that the continuity patterns based on the *official offense seriousness typology* were somewhat different from those found for the 1942 and 1949 Cohort patterns based on the the self-report dichotomy. The signs for both drug offender groups were negative and the largest positive correlation (.3941), an indication of career continuity, was for inner city non-drug offenders, secondly for non-inner city non-drug offenders. This is, of course, consistent with the data presented in Table 9.2, where we revealed that there was little continuity for drug offender types between the juvenile and adult periods. The continuity that has been found has been based simply on overall offense seriousness as shown in other tables and in the lower right hand segment of Table 9.5.

All of this leads us to perhaps the most important set of data in this chapter, Diagrams 9.4A, 9.4B, 9.4C, and 9.4D, which represent the position of members of the 1955 Cohort in the official records offense typology. This, as we have said, is the first of our cohorts to have had much contact with the police for drug offenses.

Diagrams 9.4A and 9.4B contain only those 1955 Cohort members who had had at least one police contact for a drug offense as a juvenile or as a young adult. There was little movement (only 20%) away from serious offense types between the juvenile and adult periods among those drug offenders who lived in the inner city as juveniles (Diagram 9.4A) but

DIAGRAM 9.4 JUVENILE OFFICIAL RECORD OFFENSE TYPE VS. ADULT OFFICIAL OFFENSE TYPE: 1955 COHORT

INNER CITY

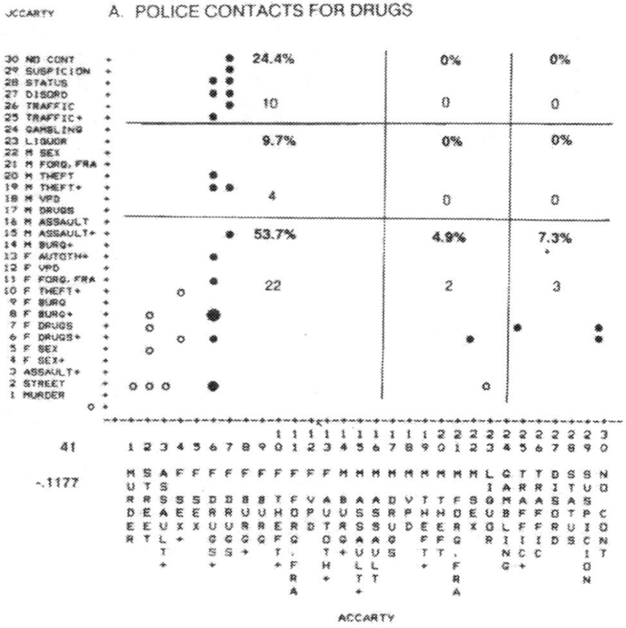

JCCARTY
A. POLICE CONTACTS FOR DRUGS
30 NO CONT
29 SUSPICION
28 STATUS
27 DISORD
26 TRAFFIC
25 TRAFFIC+
24 GAMBLING
23 LIQUOR
22 M SEX
21 M FORG, FRA
20 M THEFT
19 M THEFT+
18 M VPD
17 M DRUGS
16 M ASSAULT
15 M ASSAULT+
14 M BURG+
13 F AUTOTH+
12 F VPD
11 F FORG, FRA
10 F THEFT+
9 F BURG
8 F BURG+
7 F DRUGS
6 F DRUGS+
5 F SEX
4 F SEX+
3 ASSAULT+
2 STREET
1 MURDER
24.4%
10
0%
0
0%
0
9.7%
4
0%
0
0%
0
53.7%
22
4.9%
2
7.3%
3
41
-.1177
ACCARTY

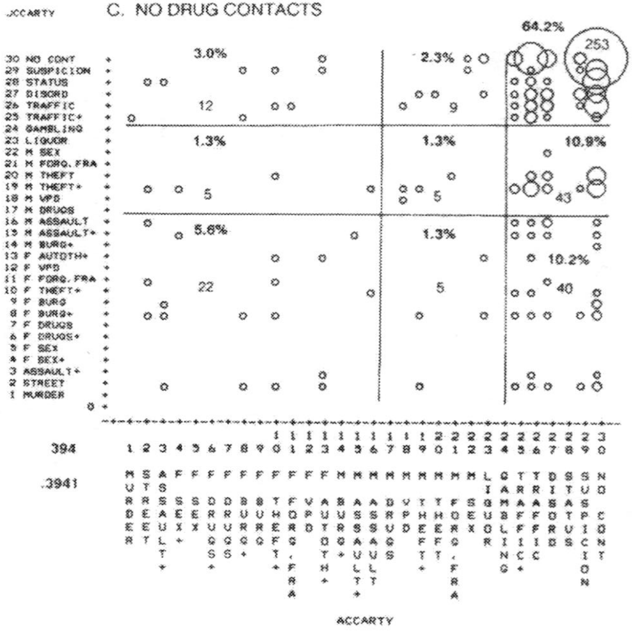

JCCARTY
C. NO DRUG CONTACTS
30 NO CONT
29 SUSPICION
28 STATUS
27 DISORD
26 TRAFFIC
25 TRAFFIC+
24 GAMBLING
23 LIQUOR
22 M SEX
21 M FORG, FRA
20 M THEFT
19 M THEFT+
18 M VPD
17 M DRUGS
16 M ASSAULT
15 M ASSAULT+
14 M BURG+
13 F AUTOTH+
12 F VPD
11 F FORG, FRA
10 F THEFT+
9 F BURG
8 F BURG+
7 F DRUGS
6 F DRUGS+
5 F SEX
4 F SEX+
3 ASSAULT+
2 STREET
1 MURDER
3.0%
12
2.3%
9
64.2%
253
1.3%
5
1.3%
5
10.9%
43
5.6%
22
1.3%
5
10.2%
40
394
.3941
ACCARTY

NON-INNER CITY

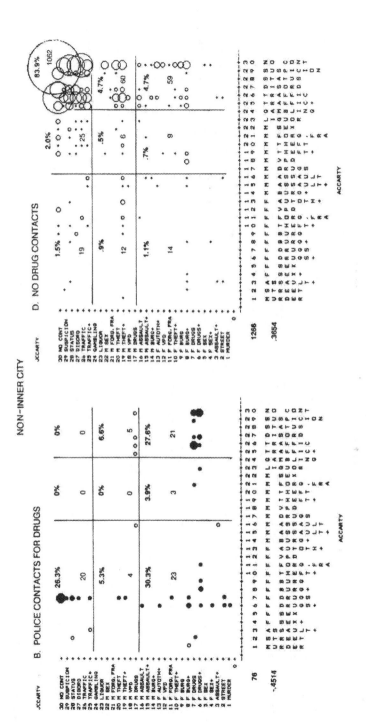

100% of those who were in non-serious offense types as juveniles had moved into the drug offender category as young adults. On the other hand, there was considerable desistance (55%) from serious career types among those who resided in non-inner city neighborhoods (Diagram 9.4B) and, although more than half of the drug offenders had moved into less serious offender types, 70% of those in non-serious offender types had moved into the drug offender category as adults. Of course, as the cohort members in Diagrams 9.4A and 9.4B were categorized, everyone must fall into a drug offender or even more serious type (which also includes drug offenses) as either a juvenile or adult. Diagrams 9.4A and 9.4B reveal that only 6.6% of the entire cohort had official contacts for drug offenses. Desistance from serious offender types as young adults was lowest (continuity was the highest) for those who resided in the inner city. Although those non-inner city cohort members who were felony-level drug offender types as juveniles had a high desistance rate as young adults, those who resided in the inner city had a lower desistance rate. Most obvious is the fact that felony-level young adult drug offenders came from a variety of juvenile offender types but those in the inner city were from more serious juvenile types than were those from other types of neighborhoods.

Perusal of these four tables illustrates the diversity in juvenile/adult continuity that is found by controlling for place of juvenile residence and by whether or not a cohort member has had police contacts for drug offenses. Diagrams 9.4C and 9.4D enable us to see how neighborhood does, without involving the drug nexus, seem to influence offender career continuity. Diagram 9.4C reveals that two-thirds of those cohort members who were in serious offender types as juveniles were in non-serious offender types as adults. Less than 5% of the 394 cohort members in this diagram had serious career continuity in comparison with 50% in Diagram 9.4A. Cohort members included in Diagram 9.4D, those residents in neighborhoods outside the inner city as juveniles, comprised 70.7% of the cohort. Those who were in serious offender types as juveniles desisted from this behavior in 90% of the cases as young adults. Only 2% of the cohort members in Diagram 9.4D were in serious offender types as adults and only half of 1% of those 1,267 cohort members had serious career continuity. With or without drug involvement, the impact of the inner city's neighborhood milieu on offender type continuity is considerable.

If we turn again to Official Offense Seriousness Scores, a variable which represents the seriousness of offenses weighted by the frequency of these offenses, the pattern is consistent regardless of the variable used for dichotomization (see Table 9.5). When this seriousness of career measure is used rather than the typology rank, the highest correlations are found for inner city drug offenders, .4807. This is, in part, an artifact of the law; drug contacts were considered felonies and thus were given a high rank on the seriousness scale. Moreover, and this is important in evaluating other research which places great emphasis on the delinquency/crime/drug nexus, the multitude of drug offenses included in careers, perhaps many single offenses in an hour, generate artificial linkages as a product of the illegality of drugs from manufacture to consumption. This is not to say that illegal drugs are not a pressing social and health problem or that drug-related crimes from theft to murder should be disregarded. We must, however, consider shocking statistics in their context. That has been one of our major concerns.

Conclusion

While a total career seriousness measure or a measure of juvenile/adult continuity tends to focus attention on drug users/offenders, the difference between inner city and other neighborhoods for drug users/offenders and non-users/offenders suggests that place of socialization is as important as drug use in producing different patterns of continuity. This lends very strong support for social structure explanations of how delinquency and crime are generated and how these behaviors develop into career continuity. It is questionable that it provides a basis for directing our attention to drug users/offenders rather than to serious inner city offenders, if attention is to be focused on a target group. That is really a different matter because one could also construct a rationale for focusing attention on drug users/offenders who work in the central business district but who reside in the suburbs (or in glitzy inner-city dwelling units) but hold such responsible positions in society that their drug use presents a greater threat than that of the inner city poorest of the poor, those whose only organizing principle in life is the search for funds with which to become "high." Does "cracking" down on drugs provide the poor with another life theme?

The delinquency/crime problem, insofar as it is one of dealing with all-around street offenders, is one of how to deal with those who, as a consequence of their antecedents and ascribed/achieved characteristics, have not been integrated into the larger society. This calls attention to social process types of explanations and how they may be used in the construction of programs which foster integration rather than alienation. Many persons are again shifting to the position that to solve the crime problem involves looking at delinquents and criminals as products of society rather than as kinds of people.

We see the question of how offender type distribution and continuit varies with drug involvement and neighborhood of residence as a question of theoretical importance. Given that the structure of the community i related to and productive of patterns of delinquency and crime and type of delinquents and criminals, and that drug users are far more widel dispersed throughout the community than are those with police contact for offenses, a combination of social structure and social process theory will be needed as the basis for generating testable hypotheses about the relationship of drugs to delinquency and crime.

What seems most apparent, considering the analyses that we have conducted, is that there is a linkage between drugs and a proportion of the ordinary street crime in the inner city but that this linkage is present to a more limited extent or is almost absent for non-inner city areas. Whei the link is present outside the inner city, it probably involves a different type of crime.

The error that many have made is to look for *the* link rather than how different kinds of links develop. That this is what we must do should no be surprising considering the structure or organization of society, its relationship to the ecology of the city, and variation in social processes that are related to the demographic composition of neighborhoods Without this sort of theoretical understanding, we could continue to seek answers, as we have done in the past, to a simple but unanswerable question like the "cause" of crime.

Note

1. *Patterns of Drug Use and Their Relation to Improving Prediction of Patterns of Delinquency and Crime* (Shannon, 1988), National Institute of Justice Grant 87-IJ-CX-0045.

Chapter 10

SUMMARY AND CONCLUSIONS

Summary

After an introductory chapter outlining the social structural approach which guided our research, we turned to the second chapter, a picture of the ecology of the city and how arenas for different types and patterns of delinquency and crime developed, not only in the inner city but in some peripheral areas. These arenas provided a setting for the early learning of rationalizations for behavior that the larger society considers inimical to public order and safety and surely a threat to private and public property. Delinquency and crime have become traditions in these areas. Their residents have no more control over delinquency and crime than do citizens from other types of neighborhoods who are equally disdainful of the white collar offenses which may be every day phenomena in their worlds of work.

Social structure and social process theories of how delinquency and crime are generated, particularly in the inner city and interstitial areas, were supported by a variety of analyses described in the first two chapters. While the findings do not excuse those who commit offenses as juveniles, much less as adults, they provide a basis for understanding juvenile delinquency and adult crime. They focus attention on how delinquency and crime are generated among a large proportion of the youthful population in some neighborhoods, how there is a high incidence of some offenses in some neighborhoods, and why severe sanctions have only a minimal impact on the number of offenders and the number of offenses which take place.

Our numerous earlier attempts to predict adult criminal or non-criminal status from juvenile status as delinquent or non-delinquent in the three birth cohorts found that juveniles who were at the extremely serious end of the continuum of any index of misbehavior or involvement in the justice system in their early years had a high probability of continuity into the adult period. Those who had few or no police contacts as juveniles were far less likely to have become involved in the justice system as adults. There were, however, so many errors, such high proportions of false positives (persons who committed offenses as juveniles but not as adults) and so many false negatives (persons who did not commit offense as juveniles but did so as adults), that we could not recommend that the findings be used in any decision-making process which would involve intervention in the lives of juveniles, i.e., more interference than what might normally be expected in the course of referring Part I or felony-level serious offenders to the juvenile court.

Interviewing a sample of the 1942 and 1949 Cohort members had shed considerable light on how juveniles perceived their misbehaviors as having developed during their formative years as part of the process of social interaction at home, at school, and at work. Most had not become involved with the justice system as a consequence of sheer malicious intent but as a product of their search for fun and new experiences and a means of expressing themselves. As they grew older most ceased to behave in such a fashion as to become involved with the justice system for serious offenses. They had changed their self-concepts and rethought their notions of proper behavior as had their friends who had been involved in juvenile misbehavior.

In our larger metropolitan areas there are neighborhoods in which far over half of the youth are unemployed. In these neighborhoods crimes against property and crimes of violence related to the control of the illegal means to making money with which to purchase needed goods (even un-needed goods such as drugs) undoubtedly make up a larger proportion of the offenses and account for a larger proportion of the offenders than in Racine. The media suggest that delinquency and crime in Racine are becoming more and more like the metropolitan model. Only another cohort will tell us how much that is really the case.

The homogeneity of Racine's spatial units, neighborhoods, census tracts, police grids, and natural areas, was greater at the extremes of distributions (the inner city and transitional areas and the peripheral high SES areas) but areas in the middle tended to be more heterogeneous. How patterns of delinquency and crime shifted with the changing social organization and ecological structure of the city was described in the third chapter, indicating that the relationship between delinquency and crime and changing characteristics of spatial units was not as straightforward as expected.

Nevertheless, a variety of analyses indicated that, cohort by cohort, no matter which system of spatial units or measures of justice system involvement was used, the inner city areas were developing continuing patterns of delinquency and crime as were those persons who resided in the inner city. This was referred to as the hardening of the inner city.

Moreover, multivariate analyses indicated that prior rates of delinquency and crime had a greater effect on continuing delinquency and crime rates than did the ecological variables in themselves. In sum, this chapter further focused our attention on structural variables as represented by neighborhood and cohort variation from 1950 to 1960 to 1970.

This drew us to Chapter 4 and a more detailed analysis of changing measures of delinquency and crime with emphasis on variation in the delinquency and crime producing (DCP) characteristics of neighborhoods as well as their historic rates of delinquency and crime. We next attempted to go even further with the idea of a snowballing effect following high rates of police contacts, referrals, and then court dispositions, the latter culminating in increasingly high severity of sanctions.

Sanctions in the inner city would, it was hypothesized, be disproportionately higher than those in areas successively further from the inner city, i.e., higher SES neighborhoods. Each stage in the justice system from contact to sanctions should reveal increasingly disproportional involvement in high DCP and high delinquency and crime rate neighborhoods. Although the cumulative nature of careers did reveal that intervention was more often followed by continuity than discontinuity, the evidence was strong only if inner city and other neighborhoods were compared. For example, 52.3% of all highly sanctioned juvenile cohort members were from inner city neighborhoods although only 24.4% of the cohort resided there as juveniles, 46.8% and 20.2% for adults. Disproportional sanctioning was highest for inner city Non-Whites followed by inner city Whites.

Since the development of serious careers in delinquency and crime could not be attributed entirely to the nature of inner city vs. other neighborhoods, we went on to the next step as described in Chapter 5 and investigated variation in the background (demographic) characteristics and life experiences (from interviews) of cohort members within various types of neighborhoods (ecological variation). The demographic variable (race/ethnicity) has an ecological distribution, sex does not, and the life experience variables had some ecological variation but also varied within types of neighborhoods.

The social process variables accounted for over half of the variance in some juvenile and adult measures of career seriousness for Non-Whites, a pattern of variable effects that differed with sex and race, significant but lesser amounts (circa 30-40%) of the variance for White males. They demonstrated that life experiences or combinations of experiences had different effects in their relationship to delinquency and crime in the worlds of males and females and the worlds of Whites and Non-Whites. Not even high school graduation (no significant effects for Non-White official seriousness scores) had the same effects across groups, all things considered. These interview variables generally accounted for more of the inner city variances than in other neighborhoods.

The proportion of Non-White and White differences in delinquency seriousness accounted for by life experiences were about the same during the juvenile period but more of the adult differences were accounted for among the Non-Whites. Unfortunately, it is difficult to say that the variables with the most consistent significant effects (NODIPLOMA, SELF617 [concept], and ADJFRTR [juvenile friends in trouble]) are entirely antecedent to career offender scores, particularly for the juvenile period.

When interview data were combined with juvenile delinquency scores (Chapter 5, Table 5.8) we saw that more than two-thirds of the variance in official adult seriousness scores for males, White or Non-White, was accounted for. From half to three-fourths of the self-report seriousness of inner city males, White or Non-White, was also accounted for by these variables, less for White males who resided in other neighborhoods and even less for all females residing in comparable neighborhoods.

What this commenced to add up to was that juvenile males from the inner city who had had serious official or self-report careers in delinquency and who had had friends in trouble with the police (antecedent or concurrently with their delinquency) who had not graduated from high school, who had access to an automobile, with some race differences in effects, had a greater likelihood of continuing into adult crime than did females or Whites from other neighborhoods (there were few Blacks in other neighborhoods). This is not new to those who have been involved in delinquency research but it does re-focus our attention on the necessity of developing a more detailed theory of how structural and processual variables should be combined to account for a greater proportion of the relationship between juvenile and adult encounters with the justice system.

The findings in Chapter 5 pointed to the importance of integrating juveniles into the larger society through school and into meaningful work that minimized associations with delinquent and criminal role models. Chapter 6, however, indicated that how the justice system functioned might be impeding the integration rather than facilitating the integration of juveniles even more than we had yet recognized. Institutionalization for a felony, it turned out, was more likely to have as its consequence another felony than were less punitive responses. Furthermore, the untoward effects of early institutionalization seemed to wear off slowly compared to the effects of less severe sanctions. The results of our various analyses led to the conclusion that greater use of institutionalization would probably do little to lower the overall delinquency and crime rate--certainly not a new conclusion but this time one based on longitudinal data.

Combinations of demographic, ecological, behavioral, and experiential (justice system) variables accounted for as much as 57% of future offense seriousness for the 1955 Cohort at the ninth police contact, lower proportions for the other cohorts or the combined cohorts but, no matter what we did, age at first police contact had the greatest and most consistent effects, followed by race, then sex. Some have seen this as support for labeling but it is problematical whether self-labeling or official labeling is the product of early contact, perhaps both depending on how representatives of the justice system interacted with the juvenile offender.

Early age, it would seem, told us little more in an explanatory sense, than did the early Philadelphia research or our earliest analyses dating back to the 1970s. Neither number nor severity of prior sanctions had effects of sufficient impact to more than suggest that number of prior sanctions was slightly more important than was their severity. If labeling was a major explanatory variable, shouldn't number of sanctions have had considerable impact on future seriousness? It did not and even suggested that number of sanctions, as opposed to their severity, had a slight deterrent effect.

When age at contact and race were eliminated as independent variables, total prior offense seriousness, number of prior sanctions (court interventions), and inner city residence produced the only significant effects but only 9% to 15% of the variance in future offense seriousness was accounted for. In other words, there was still no evidence that increasing severity of sanctions would be effective in delinquency and crime control. Increased institutionalization would only further accelerate the acquisition of delinquent and criminal patterns of behavior for, even if it had a temporary impact on those who were institutionalized, their return to society would place them back in society with the same peers, poising them for a return to serious misbehavior and another institutional experience.

If we reflect on this acceleration in delinquent behavior, it is apparent that age of contact and race must have been quite important explanatory variables. Was age at contact important simply because it was an indicator of early delinquent activity and early learning rather than evidence of early labeling? Or are early police contacts a product of the way of life of inner city males or, even more, of inner city Non-Whites? Do we hear middle, upper middle, and upper class youth referred to a being street-wise? Unless we asked police officers a series of question about how much a part name- and face-recognition played in the attention that they paid to youth in their patrol areas, it would be difficult to perceive the data as evidence for labeling. Looking back, the interview questions on self-concept were not sufficiently time- and event-related to support an argument for self-labeling.

At this point in our research (Chapter 7) we turned to what has been a provoking topic for many years, criminal typology. We were concerned about the possibility of using typology as an approach to better categorizing cohort members than had been possible with unidimensional measures. A variety of offender typologies were developed which not only had considerable heuristic value but which also enabled us to place people in relatively discrete types based on their miscreant behavior and their justice system experiences. Some were what could be called constructed typologies and some were computer-generated. All enabled us to delineate that very small proportion of the cohorts (less than 5%) who were responsible for a large proportion (circa 80%) of the felonies such as burglary and robbery.

In the next chapter we continued to explore typology development, turning back to types based on the nature of the offenses which characterized an offender's career. These types were arrayed so that it was possible to see not only the frequency of the offenses which had placed a person in a type but the frequency with which each cohort member had had police contacts for all other reasons. This highlighted what we had referred to as the heterogeneity of delinquent and criminal careers.

Our major question remained. Would types permit better prediction of adult careers from juvenile careers than did the unidimensional measures? It was apparent that they did not as long as they were manipulated as though each type had a position on an interval scale, but that was not the end because it appeared that continuity was more complex. This led us to further examination of types, the place of juvenile drug offenders and other types of offenders in terms of their relationship to adult offenders, and the possibility that drug offenses have a catalytic role in career continuation beyond the behavior to increased justice system involvement upon recognition that drugs have played a role in one's career.

Chapter 9 leaves no question about the existence of a drug and delinquency/crime nexus but still does not permit causal inferences. First police contacts for drugs appear in the careers of cohort members before and after ordinary street offenses. That those who had official police contacts for drug offenses had more serious offender careers than did other cohort members is unquestioned (even with drug offenses removed) and that a large proportion of the officially recorded serious offenders had drug offenses in the panoply of offenses in their careers is unquestioned. Henry Ford once wrote, "If you will study the history of almost any criminal you will find that he is an inveterate cigarette smoker." But cigarette smoking is probably no more the cause of crime than are drugs. Even a common cause is problematical.

Unfortunately for those who see the war on drugs as the war which will take an enormous bite out of crime, our analyses revealed that the role of drugs in delinquency/crime continuity is not simple. What that role might be became more complex through the introduction of controls for neighborhood of socialization and whether or not respondents had had a police contact for a drug offense. Rather than a link between drugs and delinquency/crime, there are probably different kinds of links, some more stable than others. In some cases the link between drugs and delinquency/crime or drugs and career continuity is only there because the use of specified drugs is a crime.

In the end one could develop a rationale for focusing attention on drug users/offenders who work in the inner city but reside in peripheral, high SES neighborhoods, as well as on serious offenders who reside in the inner city.

Conclusion

Our arrival in Racine in the late 1950s enabled us to focus on change as it occurred over the years in the organization of production, in the ecology of the city, and in various types of areas (by place of offense and place of residence of offenders), particularly inner city vs. other neighborhoods as well as in rates of delinquency and crime in the city as a whole. As the project continued, we found that beyond the social structural changes and increasing delinquency and crime rates there were changes in the public's perception of the delinquency/crime problems. This had undoubtedly become an additional variable with its own effects on changing rates and spatial differences in changing rates of delinquency and crime.

For those who have only recently defined delinquency and crime as problems we must point out that in the *Racine Journal-News*, June 9, 1913 (price three cents) a front page headline "'Bad Boy' Again in Hands of Law--Richard T. ____, 6, Arrested Many Times--Father Also in Court," prefaces an article which asks, "What shall be done...His ambition is to

run away from home, enter stores and private homes and carry awa
anything that suits his fancy."

On January 12, 1961, former President Herbert Hoover, in an addres
at the Dedication of the Herbert Hoover Dike in Florida, stated, "Thi
Nation, founded in strength will not decline or fall if we continue t
remedy our slump in morals with its trail of crime and corruption." Doe
not this remind us of today's headlines, 1991?

The media are filled not only with concern about juvenile delinquenc
and adult crime but with stories by investigative journalists which describ
its links to drugs. It is appropriate to note that an article in th
Smithsonian (Tate, 1989) pointed out that smoking tobacco has had a lon
history of criticism commencing on ecclesiastical grounds in the Fifteent
Century. In the 1830s temperance workers argued that it (tobacco
created a "morbid or diseased thirst that could only be satisfied by th
whiskey jug or brandy bottle." In addition to a multitude of diseases fo
which it was responsible, "It fostered pauperism and crime....it hac
'ruinous effects' on morality."

By contrast, during World War I tobacco was sent to Europe at th
request of General Pershing, Commander in Chief of American force
there at the time. Even children collected pennies to pay for it and th
inmates of prisons gave up their tobacco rations to help defeat th
Germans.

Changes in delinquency and crime rates must be seen in a world o
change. We have noted at considerable length that changing neighborhoo
characteristics provide the background for understanding changing spatia
patterns of delinquency and crime. We have shown that combinations o
background characteristics and experiences seem to have different effect
on cohort members depending on their race and sex and, going a ste
further, that the characteristics of different kinds of neighborhoods, th
experiences which they seem to generate, have different effects on cohor
members depending on their race and sex. In other words, we found tha
the processes by which delinquency and crime were generated varied b
neighborhood (a proxy for SES), race, and sex. Explaining human
behavior becomes even more complex when we recognize that the same
neighborhood may produce cohort members who cannot read the news and
others who are in the news because they have excelled, if not in the
professions, in other activities which are highly valued in the larger
society.

If we are to even begin to understand changing patterns of delinquency
and crime we must understand how society is organized so that various
types of early learning experiences (opportunities for social learning) are

not equally distributed by neighborhoods and to some extent within neighborhoods. Also disproportionately distributed are later formal and informal learning experiences in school, learning experiences in the neighborhood during school and before employment (which may cover a considerable period of time), learning in the job search and on the job, learning when the chances for a job seem to be fading, and the learning that takes place later in life as some people achieve positions of responsibility and trust.

In essence, we commenced with a social structure approach which utilizes various ecological or spatial representations of the distributions of institutions, populations, and life experience as a starting point. We then, in relating background and life experience data to delinquency and crime, described or at least attempted to understand how on-going social processes and their variation account for differences in delinquency and crime rates by sex, race, and neighborhood of residence.

Still, as we have seen, structural and processual variables do not account for all of the variation in delinquency and crime rates, even if we take into consideration the impact of intervening justice system experiences. The next step would involve more idiosyncratic variables than those which were measured by data collected from official sources or interviews. Beyond this there is the matter of chance, for example, chance that misbehavior was detected. It has always been our position that the stochastic nature of offender careers is based, as others have also found, on: (1) the relative lack of orderly progression in offense seriousness, even more, the relatively gradual decline in offense seriousness for most persons as their career consists more and more of traffic offenses or other less serious offenses consistent with adult roles and (2) the failure of police to detect, record, and take action on the total offender career of most offenders.

So what we have is a basic understanding of how much of the delinquency and crime is generated in selected neighborhoods with a history of structured disadvantage and a limited amount of data which indicate how processual explanations must vary somewhat on a basis of sex, race, and type of neighborhood of socialization.

We conclude that the causes of delinquency and crime are structural and processual, i.e., learned or acquired in a milieu as a consequence of group interaction, rather than based on types of people with this or that predisposition toward delinquency and crime. Delinquent acts are as normal in some settings as are non-delinquent acts in other settings. The changing patterns of delinquency and crime which have been delineated by rate differences and differences in patterns (types) of offenses are more

or less a natural outgrowth of the changing social and spatial organizatio
of society. A more precise description of how this works has bee
suggested by the dynamic and comparative dimensions of this research.

Can These Findings be Applied to Delinquency Prevention?

How may these findings guide persons on the firing line? Sinc
antecedent variable effects were inconsistent from group to group, it i
difficult to suggest how to deal with the problem of delinquency or crim
prevention in a way that cuts across groups. Attention should probabl
be focused on those groups in which delinquency rates were highest an
where there was the greatest likelihood of continuity into adult crime, i.e.
the high risk groups.

Unfortunately, most variables related to delinquency and crime in th
inner city and interstitial areas are those over which persons concerne
about delinquency prevention or reduction have no direct control. The
may verbalize the existence of predisposing neighborhood conditions ever
day but are helpless in the face of an all-pervasive milieu which has bee
there for generations, as long as social differences have existed. The
recognize that it is (in terms of the concentration of official seriousness.
self-report seriousness, and offense seriousness/intervention) a matter o
focusing attention on inner city males if the groups with the highes
delinquency rates are to be the target of any program, i.e., any progran
aimed at ordinary street crime. That involves deciding whether there i
even a remote chance of manipulating some of the crucial causa
variables.

The development of opportunities to integrate juveniles into the large
society should be a major concern of programs designed for inner cit
neighborhoods, but (to the extent that delinquency is a problem in othe
neighborhoods of the city) programs should, as they have in the past, be
oriented toward keeping juveniles in the school system.

We had earlier found that the 6 to 12 year olds (who had very low
delinquency rates during the school year compared with other youth unde
21) showed proportionally larger increases in delinquency during the
summer months than did those of either the 13 to 17 or 18 to 20 groups,
although both of the latter had sufficiently high summer-time delinquenc
and youthful crime increases to be of concern, particularly among the
inner city youth who already had higher police contact rates. Whateve
the school adds to the generation of delinquency as an arena fo
misbehavior, its integrating force appears to exceed its negative effects.

The simple fact that cohort police contact rates for juveniles ages 13 through 17 have been higher during the summer months than during the school year by almost 25% suggests that the school, while a source of some rationalizations for delinquency and ideas about delinquent behavior, i.e., a source of learning, also plays an integrating role and that role is much less direct during the summer. Not only did youth 13 to 17 have a higher police contact rate during both the school year and the summer months than younger or older youth, regardless of the type of neighborhood in which they lived (with few exceptions), but their summer-month (non-school year) rate was higher than that during the school year.

Studies which have either shown that income is a product of education or that there is no one-to-one relationship of education to income have usually been flawed by failure to consider the relevant related variables or to control for race/ethnicity, sex, and parental socioeconomic status. However difficult it may be to integrate persons of all ages and backgrounds into urban, industrial society, we can determifie what the school system will be like. We can reprogram and modify the school system even when we find modification of the larger social structure more difficult. Some social institutions are more difficult to penetrate but we do have a basis for making the school a major Federal concern. This means more than calling for excellence. It means paying for excellence.

For the inner city program, however, it is probably insufficient to emphasize school retention unless retention leads to integration into the world of meaningful work. In modifying the school system we should develop better links between school and work, providing jobs for those for whom lack of a job is not only an invitation to delinquency but a necessity for survival. On the other hand, the error has sometimes been to conclude that jobs in themselves will reduce delinquency and crime rates when it is apparent that early work has different effects on different groups. Work as at least a partial solution to the problem is tied to the question of what various types of jobs mean in terms of experiences and what they are believed to lead to in the future. Summer employment in a dirty, physically demanding job may have one meaning to the collegiate who wishes to toughen himself for a year of sports activity but quite a different meaning to someone who is likely to qualify for nothing more challenging in the foreseeable future, even less likely to have better opportunities as time passes.

In the end, as long as a multitude of illegal, non-conforming behaviors are perceived to be more rewarding than the forms of work available to youth and to adults, neither the verbal carrot nor the temporarily incapacitating stick will do much to reduce the rate of juvenile and adult lawbreaking.   Understanding how types and patterns of delinquency are generated and change, one of the classical problems of sociologists, should enable us to see that increasingly severe sanctions as well as most other current approaches to specific and general deterrence should be supplanted by a variety of societal changes geared as much as possible to prevention rather than punitive reaction.

It is difficult for those who have perceived themselves as facing a life of unemployment or at best one "dead end" job after another to react with enthusiasm to what is usually offered to them as a "job." Whether the perceptions of those who have been socialized in the inner city are entirely accurate or not is an academic question. Inner city youth grow up to perceive and react to the world differently than do the middle and upper classes because their part of the world and their life experiences are different. This theme has been developed at length in Currie (1985).

We must also realize that what makes for integration into the larger society differs from group to group within the same milieu, just as the process of exclusion appears to be working differently from group to group, within and between milieus.

Above all, we must remember that we are dealing with people who are the products of society, who are behaving in a manner which seems as reasonable to them as our behavior does to us. If we wish them to change, we must demonstrate that other patterns of behavior are more reasonable because they are more rewarding. In this way most ordinary delinquency and crime no longer has the same attraction. The problem is even more complex when those who have been integrated into the larger society and have positions of responsibility and varying degrees of financial success still betray the trust that has been placed in them.

We have been concerned about the multi-billion dollar cost of repairing the damage that has been done to the Savings and Loan institutions and many months of Congressional and Executive wrangling have been devoted to it. Much has been said about how the S and L crisis was a product of the system. That may well be the case, but juvenile delinquency and adult crime of the type that is dealt with day-by-day is even more a product of the system. We, as a society, have not addressed this problem and its impact on how inner city and less advantaged persons view the larger society which is so eager to chastise its less advantaged miscreants. Let us at least be as understanding as we have been of high-level, trust-breaking offenses by those who were not in poverty.

References

Adler, Freda, 1975. *Sisters in Crime: The Rise of the New Female Criminal*. New York: McGraw-Hill.

Ageton, Suzanne S. and Delbert S. Elliott, 1974. "The Effects of Legal Processing on Delinquent Orientations," *Social Problems* 22:87-100.

Akers, Ronald L., 1973. *Deviant Behavior: A Social Learning Approach*. Belmont: Wadsworth Publishing.

Anderson, Kathleen, 1984. "A Comparison of Two Offense Seriousness Scales." Iowa City: Iowa Urban Community Research Center, 28 pp.

Arnold, William R., 1971. "Race and Ethnicity Relative to Other Factors in Juvenile Court Dispositions," *American Journal of Sociology* 77:211-227.

Austin, Roy, 1982. "Women's Liberation and Increase in Minor, Major, and Occupational Offenses," *Criminology* 20:407-430.

Ball-Rokeach, Sandra J., 1973. "Values and Violence: A Test of the Subculture of Violence Thesis," *American Sociological Review* 38:736-749.

Bernstein, Ilene N., William R. Kelly, and Patricia A. Doyle, 1977. "Societal Reaction to Deviants: The Case of Criminal Defendants," *American Sociological Review* 42:743-755.

Black, Donald J., 1970. "Production of Crime Rates," *American Sociological Review* 35:733-748.

Blau, Judith R. and Peter M. Blau, 1982. "The Cost of Inequality: Metropolitan Structure and Violent Crime," *American Sociological Review* 47:114-129.

Block, Richard, 1979. "Community, Environment, and Violent Crime," *Criminology* 17:46-57.

Blumstein, Alfred and Jacqueline Cohen, 1979. "Estimating Individual Crime Rates from Arrest Records," *Journal of Criminal Law and Criminology* 70:571-585.

Blumstein, Alfred, Jacqueline Cohen, Susan E. Martin, and Michael H. Tonry, (eds.), 1983. *Research in Sentencing: The Search for Reform*. Washington, D.C.: National Academy Press.

Blumstein, Alfred, Jacqueline Cohen, Jeffrey Roth, and Christy Visher (eds), 1986. *Criminal Careers and "Career Criminals."* Washington: National Academy Press.

Bordua, David J., 1961. "Delinquent Subcultures: Sociological Interpretations of Gang Delinquency," *The Annals of the American Academy of Political and Social Science* 38:120-136.

Brennan, Tim, 1980. *Multivariate Taxonomical Classification for Criminal Justice Research.* Final Report to the National Institute of Justice, Office of Research Evaluation Methods, Project Number 78-NI-AX- 0065.

Burgess, Ernest W., 1925. *The Urban Community.* Chicago: The University of Chicago Press.

Bursik, Robert J., Jr., and Jim Webb, 1982. "Community Change and Patterns of Delinquency," *American Journal of Sociology* 88:24-42.

Chaiken, Jan M. and Marcia R. Chaiken, 1982. *Varieties of Criminal Behavior.* Santa Monica, California: Rand.

Chaiken, Marcia and Jan M. Chaiken, 1984. "Offender Types and Public Policy," *Crime and Delinquency* 30:195-225.

Chilton, Roland J., 1964. "Continuity in Delinquency Area Research: A Comparison of Studies for Baltimore, Detroit, and Indianapolis," *American Sociological Review* 29:71-83.

Chilton, Roland J. and Gerald E. Markle, 1972. "Family Disruption, Delinquent Conduct and the Effect of Sub- Classification," *American Sociological Review* 37:93-99.

Chiricos, Theodore G., Phillip D. Jackson and Gordon P. Waldo, 1972. "Inequality in the Imposition of a Criminal Label," *Social Problems* 19:553-572.

Clark, John P. and Eugene P. Wenninger, 1962. "Socio- Economic Class and Area as Correlates of Illegal Behavior among Juveniles," *American Sociological Review* 27:826-834.

Cloward, Richard A. and Lloyd E. Ohlin, 1960. *Delinquency and Opportunity: A Theory of Delinquent Gangs.* New York: Free Press.

Cohen, Albert K., 1955. *Delinquent Boys: The Culture of the Gang.* New York: Macmillan Publishing Co., Inc.

Cook, Philip J., 1980. "Research in Criminal Deterrence: Laying the Groundwork for the Second Decade," in Norval Morris and Michael Tonry (eds.), *Crime and Justice, Vol. 2.* Chicago: The University of Chicago Press, pp. 211-268.

Currie, Elliott, 1985. *Confronting Crime: An American Challenge.* New York: Pantheon Books.

DeFleur, Melvin and Richard Quinney, 1966. "A Reformulation of Sutherland's Differential Association and a Strategy for Empirical Verification," *Journal of Research in Crime and Delinquency* 3:1-11.

Elliott, Delbert S. and Suzanne S. Ageton, 1980. "Reconciling Race and Class Differences in Self- Reported and Official Estimates of Delinquency," *American Sociological Review* 45:95-110.

Elliott, Delbert S., David H. Huizinga, and Suzanne S. Ageton, 1985. *Explaining Delinquency and Drug Use.* Beverly Hills: Sage.

Elliott, Delbert S. and Harwin L. Voss, 1974. *Delinquency and Dropout.* Lexington: D.C. Heath and Co., Lexington Books.

Empey, LaMar T., 1978. *American Delinquency: Its Meaning and Construction.* Homewood: The Dorsey Press.

Erlanger, Howard S., 1979. "Estrangement, Machismo and Gang Violence," *Social Science Quarterly* 60:235-248.

Ferdinand, Theodore and Elmer Luchterhand, 1962. "Inner City Youth, the Police, the Juvenile Court and Justice," *Social Problems* 18:510-517.

Ferdinand, Theodore N. and Elmer C. Luchterhand, 1970. "Inner-city Youths, the Police, the Juvenile Court, and Justice," *Social Problems* 17:510-527.

Ferracuti, Frances, Simon Dinitz and Esperanza Acosta de Brenes, 1975. *Delinquents and Nondelinquents in the Puerto Rican Slum Culture.* Columbus: Ohio State University Press.

Giallombardo, Rose, 1980. "Female Delinquency," in Schichor, David and Delos H. Kelly (eds.) *Critical Issues in Juvenile Delinquency.* Lexington: Lexington Books, D.C. Heath and Co., pp. 63-82.

Gibbons, Don C. 1965. "Two Candidate Typologies," Chapter 3, *Changing the Lawbreaker.* Englewood Cliffs: Prentice Hall.

_____, 1975. "Offender Typologies--Two Decades Later," *British Journal of Criminology* 15:140-156.

_____, 1982. "Patterns of Crime and Criminal Behavior," Chapter 10 in *Society, Crime, and Criminal Behavior.* Englewood Cliffs, N.J.: Prentice Hall.

Gibbs, Jack P., 1977. "Social Class, Deterrence, and Perspectives on Social Order," *Social Forces* 56:408- 432.

Gillin, John L., 1933. *Social Psychology.* New York: Appleton-Century Co., Inc.

Glaser, Daniel, 1956. "Criminality Theories and Behavioral Images," *American Journal of Sociology* 61:433-444.

Gottfredson, Don M., 1970. "Assessment and Prediction Methods in Crime and Delinquency," in James E. Teele (ed.), *Juvenile Delinquency*. Itasca, Illinois: F. E. Peacock, pp. 401-424.

Gottfredson, Don M. and Michael Tonry (eds.), 1987. *Prediction and Classification*. Chicago: The University of Chicago Press.

Green, Edward, 1970. "Race, Social Status and Criminal Arrest," *American Sociological Review* 35:476-490.

Greenberg, David F. (ed.), 1978. *Corrections and Punishment*, Beverly Hills: Sage Publications.

Greenberg, David, Ronald C. Kessler, and Charles H. Logan, 1979. "A Panel Model of Crime Rates and Arrest Rates," *American Sociological Review* 44:843-850.

Greenwood, Peter W., Joan Petersilia, and Franklin R. Zimring, 1980. *Age, Crime, and Sanctions: The Transition from Juvenile to Adult Court*. Santa Monica: Rand.

Greenwood, Peter W., Allan Abrahamse, and Franklin Zimring, 1984. *Factors Affecting Sentence Severity for Young Adult Offenders*. Santa Monica: Rand.

Hindelang, Michael J., Travis Hirschi, and Joseph G. Weis, 1979. "Correlates of Delinquency: The Illusion of Discrepancy Between Self-Report and Official Measures," *American Sociological Review* 44:995-1014.

_____, 1981. *Measuring Delinquency*. Beverly Hills: Sage.

Hirschi, Travis, 1969. *Causes of Delinquency*. Berkeley: University of California Press.

Hirschi, Travis and Hanan C. Selvin, 1967. *Delinquency Research: An Appraisal of Analytic Methods*. New York: The Free Press.

Hopkins, Andrew, 1976. "Imprisonment and Recidivism: A Quasi-Experimental Study," *Journal of Research in Crime and Delinquency* 13:13-32.

Hoyt, Homer, 1939. *The Structure and Growth of Residential Neighborhoods in American Cities*. Washington: Federal Housing Administration.

Jensen, Gary F., 1976. "Race, Achievement and Delinquency: A Further Look at Delinquency in a Birth Cohort," *American Journal of Sociology* 82:379-387.

Jensen, Gary F. and Dean G. Rojek, 1980. *Delinquency: A Sociological View*. Lexington, D.C. Heath.

Jessor, Richard and Shirley Jessor, 1977. *Problem Behavior and Psychosocial Development: A Longitudinal Study of Youth*. New York: Academic Press.

Johnstone, John W.D., 1978. "Social Class, Social Areas and Delinquency," *Sociology and Social Research* 36:49- 72.

Kelly, Delos H., 1976. "The Role of Teachers' Nominations in the Perpetuation of Deviant Adolescent Careers," *Education* 96:209-217.

Kobrin, Solomon, Joseph Puntil and Emil Peluso, 1967. "Criteria of Status Among Street Gangs," *Journal of Research in Crime and Delinquency* 4:98-118.

Krisberg, Barry and James Austin, 1978. *The Children of Ishmael: Criminal Perspectives on Juvenile Justice*. Palo Alto, California: Mayfield.

Lab, Steven P. and William G. Doerner, "Changes in Delinquency: A Cohort Analysis," *Criminal Justice Review*, Vol. 10, 1985, pp. 1-6.

Lemert, Edwin, 1967. "The Juvenile Court - Quest and Realities." In the President's Commission on Law Enforcement and Administration of Justice, *Task Force Report: Juvenile Delinquency and Youth Crime*. Washington, D.C.: U.S. Government Printing Office.

Leopold, Nathan F., Jr., 1958. *Life Plus 99 Years*. Garden City, New York: Doubleday & Co.

Lerman, Paul, 1968. "Individual Values, Peer Values, and Subcultural Delinquency," *American Sociological Review* 33:219-235.

Liska, Allen E. and Mark Tausig, 1974. "Theoretical Interpretations of Social Class and Racial Differentials in Legal Decision-Making for Juveniles," *The Sociological Quarterly* 10:197-207.

Lizotte, Alan J., 1978. "Extra-legal Factors in Chicago's Criminal Courts: Testing the Conflict Model of Criminal Justice," *Social Problems* 25:564-580.

Mack, John, 1963. "Full-Time Miscreants, Delinquent Neighborhoods and Criminal Networks," *British Journal of Sociology* 15:38-53.

Martin, R. I. and M. W. Klein, 1965. *A Comparative Analysis of Four Measures of Delinquency Seriousness*. Los Angeles: University of Southern California, Youth Studies Center.

Martinson, Robert, 1974. "What Works? Questions and Answers about Prison Reform," *The Public Interest* 35:22- 54.

Matza, David, 1969. *Becoming Delinquent*. Englewood Cliffs: Prentice Hall.

McCaghy, Charles H., 1962. "Social Areas and the Distribution of Juvenile Delinquency in Racine, Wisconsin, 1950-1960." Unpublished M.S. thesis, University of Wisconsin.

McEachern, Alexander W. and Riva Bauzer, 1967. "Factors Related to Disposition in Juvenile Police Contacts," in M.W. Klein (ed.), Juvenile Gangs in Context. Englewood Cliffs, N.J.: Prentice Hall, Inc.

McKenzie, Roderick D., 1933. *The Metropolitan Community*. New York: McGraw-Hill.

Meehl, Paul, 1954. *Clinical vs. Statistical Prediction: A Theoretical Analysis and a Review of the Evidence*. Minneapolis: University of Minnesota Press.

Merton, Robert K., 1957. *Social Theory and Social Structure*. New York: Free Press.

Miller, Walter B., 1958. "Lower Class Culture as a Generating Milieu of Gang Delinquency," *The Journal of Social Issues* 14:5-19.

Monahan, John, 1978. "The Prediction of Violent Criminal Behavior: A Methodological Critique and Prospectus," in Alfred Blumstein, Jacqueline Cohen, and Daniel Nagin (eds.), *Deterrence and Incapacitation: Estimating the Effects of Criminal Sanctions on Crime Rates*. Washington, D.C.: National Academy of Sciences.

____, 1981. *Predicting Violent Behavior: An Assessment of Clinical Techniques*. Beverly Hills, California: Sage.

Murphy, Patrick T., 1977. *Our Kindly Parent...The State: The Juvenile Justice System and How It Works*. New York: Viking Press.

Park, Robert E., Ernest W. Burgess, and Roderick D. McKenzie, 1925. *The City*. Chicago: The University of Chicago Press.

Petersilia, Joan, 1980. "Criminal Career Research: A Review of Recent Evidence," in Norval Morris and Michael Tonry (eds.), *Crime and Justice, Vol. 2*. Chicago: The University of Chicago Press.

____, 1983. *Racial Disparities in the Criminal Justice System*. Santa Monica, Calif.: Rand Corp.

Petersilia, Joan, Susan Turner, James Kahan, and Joyce Peterson, 1985. *Granting Felons Probation: Public Risks and Alternatives*. Prepared for the National Institute of Justice, U.S. Department of Justice. Santa Monica: Rand.

Platt, Anthony, 1969. *The Child Savers*. Chicago: The University of Chicago Press.

Polk, Kenneth and Walter E. Schafer (eds.), 1972. *Schools and Delinquency*. Englewood Cliffs, N.J.: Prentice Hall.

Reiss, Alfred J., Jr., 1951. "The Accuracy, Efficiency, and Validity of a Prediction Instrument," *American Journal of Sociology* 56:552-561.

____, 1960. "Sex Offenses: The Marginal Status of the Adolescent," *Law and Contemporary Problems*. Durham, N.C.: Duke University School of Law.

Reiss, Alfred J., Jr. and A. Lewis Rhodes, 1964. "An Empirical Test of Differential Association Theory," *The Journal of Research in Crime and Delinquency* 1:5-18.

Rhodes, William, Herbert Tyson, James Weekeley, Catherine Conly, and Gustave Powell, 1982. *Developing Criteria for Identifying Career Criminals*. U.S. Department of Justice, Office of Legal Policy, Federal Justice Research Program.

Robison, Sophia M., 1936. *Can Delinquency Be Measured?* New York: Columbia University Press.

Roncek, Dennis, 1981. "Dangerous Places: Crime and Residential Environment," *Social Forces* 60:74-96.

Schmid, Calvin F. and Earle H. MacCannel, 1955. "Basic Problems, Techniques and Theory of Isopleth Mapping," *Journal of the American Statistical Association* 50:220- 239.

Schultz, LeRoy G., 1962. "Why the Negro Carries Weapons," *Journal of Criminal Law, Criminology and Police Science* 53:476-483.

Schur, Edwin, 1971. *Labelling Deviant Behavior*. Englewood Cliffs: Prentice Hall.

Sellin, Thorsten and Marvin Wolfgang, 1964. *The Measurement of Delinquency*. New York: John Wiley and Sons.

Shannon, Lyle W., 1963. "Types and Patterns of Delinquency Referral in a Middle-Sized City," *The British Journal of Criminology* July:24-36.

_____, 1964. "Types and Patterns of Delinquency in a Middle-Sized City," *The Journal of Research in Crime and Delinquency* 1:53-66.

_____, 1967. "The Distribution of Juvenile Delinquency in a Middle-Sized City," *Sociological Quarterly* 8:365-382.

_____, 1978. "A Longitudinal Study of Delinquency and Crime," Chapter 7 in Charles Welford (ed.), *Quantitative Studies in Criminology*. Beverly Hills: Sage.

_____, 1980a. "Assessing the Relationship of Adult Criminal Careers to Juvenile Careers," in Clark C. Abt (ed.), *Problems in American Social Policy Research*. Cambridge: Abt Books.

_____, 1980b. *Assessing the Relationship of Adult Criminal Careers to Juvenile Careers*. U.S. Department of Justice, Office of Juvenile Justice and Delinquency Prevention (National Criminal Justice Reference Service NCJ77744). (A 16-page, 1982 summary is also available from NCJRS.)

_____, 1982. *The Relationship of Juvenile Delinquency and Adult Crime to the Changing Ecological Structure of the City*. Final Report to the National Institute of Justice. Grant Number 79-NI-AX-0081.

_____, 1984. *The Development of Serious Criminal Careers and the Delinquent Neighborhood*. Final report to the National Institute of

Juvenile Justice and Delinquency Prevention, Grant Number 82-JN-AX-0004.

_____, 1985. "Risk Assessment vs. Real Prediction: The Prediction Problem and Public Trust," *Journal of Quantitative Criminology* 1:159-189.

_____, 1986a. "Ecological Evidence of the Hardening of the Inner City," in Simon Hakim, George F. Rengert, and Robert M. Figlio (eds.), *Metropolitan Crime Patterns*. Monsey, N.Y.: Willow Tree Press.

_____, 1986b. *A More Precise Evaluation of the Effects of Sanctions.* National Institute of Grant Number 84-IJ-CX- 0013.

_____, 1987. *Prediction and Typology Development*, National Institute of Justice Grant Number 85-IJ-CX- 0019.

_____, 1988a. *Criminal Career Continuity: Its Social Context.* New York: Human Sciences Press.

_____, 1988b. *Patterns of Drug Use and Their Relation to Improving Prediction of Patterns of Delinquency and Crime.* Progress Report to the National Institute of Justice, Grant 87-IJ-CX-0045.

Shaw, Clifford, 1929. *Delinquency Areas.* Chicago: The University of Chicago Press.

_____, 1930. *The Jack-Roller: A Delinquent Boy's Own Story.* Chicago: The University of Chicago Press.

_____, 1938. *Brothers in Crime.* Chicago: The University of Chicago Press.

Shaw, Clifford and Henry D. McKay, 1931. *Social Factors in Juvenile Delinquency.* Washington, D.C.: U.S. Government Printing Office.

_____, 1942. *Juvenile Delinquency and Urban Areas.* Chicago: The University of Chicago Press.

Shaw, Clifford and Maurice A. Moore, 1931. *The Natural History of a Delinquent Career.* Chicago: The University of Chicago Press.

Short, James F., 1968. *Gang Delinquency and Delinquent Subcultures.* New York: Harper and Row.

Short, James F., Jr. and F. Ivan Nye, 1957. "Reported Behavior as a Criterion of Deviant Behavior," *Social Problems* 5:207-213.

Short, James F. and Fred L. Strodbeck, 1965. *Group Process and Gang Delinquency.* Chicago: The University of Chicago Press.

Skogman, Wesley G., 1977. "The Changing Distribution of Big-City Crime: A Multi-City Time-Series Analysis," *Urban Affairs Quarterly* 13:33-48.

_____, 1979. "Crime in Contemporary America," Chapter 14 in Hugh Davis Graham and Fred Robert Gurr (eds.), *Violence in America: Historical and Comparative Perspectives.* Beverly Hills: Sage.

Stark, Rodney, 1987. "Deviant Places: A Theory of the Ecology of Crime," *Criminology* 25:893-909.

Steffensmeier, Darrell J. and Renee H. Steffensmeier, 1980. "Trends in Female Delinquency: An Examination of Arrest, Juvenile Court, Self-Report, and Field Data," *Criminology* 18:62-95.

Stott, D. H., 1960. "The Prediction of Delinquency from Non-Delinquent Behavior," *British Journal of Delinquency* 10:202-210.

Sutherland, Edwin H., 1939. *Principles of Criminology.* Philadelphia: J.B. Lippincott.

Tate, Cassandra, 1989. "In the 1800s Antismoking Was a Burning Issue," *Smithsonian*, 20:107-117.

Terry, Robert M., 1966. "Police Criteria in the Screening of Juvenile Offenders," *The Wisconsin Sociologist* 58:163-181.

_____, 1967a. "Discrimination in the Handling of Juvenile Offenders by Social-Control Agencies," *Journal of Research in Crime and Delinquency* 4:218-230.

_____, 1967b. "The Screening of Juvenile Offenders," *Journal of Criminal Law, Criminology and Police Science* 58:163-181.

Thomas, Charles W. and Robin J. Cage, 1977. "The Effect of Social Characteristics on Juvenile Court Dispositions," *The Sociological Quarterly* 18:237-252.

Thornberry, Terence P., 1973. "Race, Socioeconomic Status and Sentencing in the Juvenile Justice System," *Journal of Criminal Law and Criminology* 64:90-98.

Thornberry, Terence P. and Edward Sagarin (eds.), 1972. *Images of Crime: Offenders and Victims.* New York: Praeger Publishers.

Thornberry, Terence P. and R. L. Christianson, 1984. "Juvenile Justice Decision-Making as a Longitudinal Process," *Social Forces* 63:433-444.

Thrasher, Frederick M., 1936. *The Gang.* Chicago: The University of Chicago Press.

Tittle, Charles R. and Charles H. Logan, 1973. "Sanctions and Deviance: Evidence and Remaining Questions," *Law and Society Review* 371-392.

Tittle, Charles R., Wayne J. Villemez, and Douglas A. Smith, 1978. "The Myth of Social Class and Criminality," *American Sociological Review* 43:645-656.

Toby, Jackson, 1957. "The Differential Impact of Family Disorganization," *American Sociological Review* 22:502- 512.

_____, 1965. "An Evaluation of Early Identification and Intensive Treatment Programs for Predelinquents," *Social Problems* 13:160-175.

Turk, Austin T., 1962. *Adolescence and Delinquency in Urban Society.* Unpublished Ph.D. dissertation, University of Wisconsin.

_____, 1964. "Toward Construction of a Theory of Delinquency," *Journal of Criminal Law, Criminology and Police Science* 55:215-219.

Unnever, James D., Charles E. Frazier, and John C. Henretta, 1980. "Race Differences in Criminal Settings," *The Sociological Quarterly* 21:233-252.

U.S. Department of Justice, Bureau of Justice Statistics, *The National Survey of Crime Severity BJS Bulletin,* Jan. 1984.

Voss, Harwin L., 1956. *The Ecological Distribution of Juvenile Delinquency in Madison, Wisconsin.* Unpublished M.A. thesis, University of Wisconsin.

_____, 1963. "The Predictive Efficiency of the Glueck Social Prediction Tables," *The Journal of Criminal Law, Criminology and Police Science* 54:421-430.

_____, 1964. "Differential Association and Reported Delinquent Behavior: A Replication," *Social Problems* 12:78-85.

_____, 1969. "Differential Association and Containment Theory: A Theoretical Convergence," *Social Forces* 47:381-391.

Watts, A.D. and T.M. Watts, 1981. "Minorities and Urban Crime: Are They the Cause or Victims?," *Urban Affairs Quarterly* 16:423-436.

Weis, Joseph G., 1976. "Liberation and Crime: The Invention of the New Female Criminal," *Crime and Social Justice* 2:17-27.

Weis, Joseph G. and John Sederstrom, 1981. *The Prevention of Serious Delinquency.* Washington, D.C.: Department of Justice, Office of Juvenile Justice and Delinquency Prevention.

Welch, Susan, Cassia Spohn, and John Gruhl, 1985. "Convicting and Sentencing Differences Among Black, Hispanic, and White Males in Six Localities," *Justice Quarterly* 2:67-80.

Welford, Charles F., 1967. "The Prediction of Delinquency," Chapter 2 in William F. Amos and Charles Welford (eds.), *Delinquency Prevention: Theory and Practice.* Englewood Cliffs, N.J.: Prentice Hall, Inc.

_____, 1975. "Labelling Theory and Criminology," *Social Problems* 22:332-345.

Wilkins, Leslie T., 1980. "Problems with Existing Prediction Studies and Future Research Needs," *The Journal of Criminal Law & Criminology,* Vol. 71, No. 2, pp. 98-101.

Wilkinson, Karen, 1974. "The Broken Family and Juvenile Delinquency: Scientific Explanation or Ideology," *Social Problems* 21:726-739.

Williams, Jay and Martin Gold, 1972. "From Delinquent Behaviors to Official Delinquency," *Social Problems* 29:209-227.

Williams, Kirsten, 1980. "Selection Criteria for Career Criminal Programs," *The Journal of Criminal Law and Criminology*, Vol. 71, No. 2, pp. 89-93.

Wolfgang, Marvin E. and Frances Ferracuti, 1967. *The Subculture of Violence*. London: Tavistock.

Wolfgang, Marvin E., Robert M. Figlio, and Thorsten Sellin, 1972. *Delinquency in a Birth Cohort*. Chicago: The University of Chicago Press.

Young, Venetta D., 1980. "Women, Race, and Crime," *Criminology* 18:26-34

Zatz, Marjorie S., 1984. "Race, Ethnicity, and Determinate Sentencing," *Criminology* 22:147-171.

Index

A

Abrahamse, Allen, 76, 158
Acosta de Brenes, Esperanza, 12, 157
Adler, Freda, 20, 155
Adolescence, delinquency during, 23-24
Age, at first police contact, 102
   groups, continuity in police contacts by, 77-78
   variation in offense seriousness, by 35-40
   variation in number of police contacts, by, 35-40
   variation in referrals, by, 35-40
   variation in sanctions, by, 35-40
Ageton, Suzanne S., 20, 24, 41, 155, 157
Ahlgrim, John C., 1
Akers, Ronald L., 11, 155
Anderson, Kathleen, 117, 155
Arnold, William R., 76, 155
Arrest rates, relation to census tract change, 30
Associates and delinquency/crime, 24, 64-71
Attitudes toward police, 4, 6
Austin, James, 41, 159
Austin, Roy, 18, 155

Automobiles and delinquency/crime, 27-28, 64, 67

B

Ball-Rokeach, Sandra J., 44, 155
Bauzer, Riva, 76, 159
Bernstein, Ilene N., 19, 155
Black, Donald J., 155
Blau, Judith R., 41, 155
Blau, Peter M., 41, 155
Block, Richard, 12, 76, 155
Blumstein, Alfred, 45, 50, 76, 94, 155
Bordua, David J., 14, 156
Brennan, Tim, 94, 156
Burgess, Ernest W., 10, 45, 156, 160
Bursik, Robert J., Jr., 28, 156

C

Cage, Robin J., 76, 163
Career, consistency of, in neighborhood, 50-54
   continuity and drug use, 136-141
   determinants of continuity in, 89-90
   effects of sanctions on continuity, 50-53, 78-87, 146-147

M

Mack, John, 12, 159
Markle, Gerald E., 22, 156
Marriage, and delinquency/and
    crime, 67, 71
Martin, R. I., 94, 159
Martin, Susan E., 45, 76, 155
Martinson, Robert, 75, 159
Matza, David, 10, 11, 159
MacCannel, Earle H., 29, 161
McCaghy, Charles M., 1, 10,
    12, 159
McCormick, Thomas C., 1
McEachern, Alexander W., 76,
    159
McKay, Henry D., 10, 22, 25,
    162
McKenzie, Roderick D., 10,
    45, 59, 160
Meehl, Paul, 94, 160
Merton, Robert K., 14, 24, 160
Miller, Walter B., 12, 14, 24,
    160
Minority groups, density of,
    30-31
Monahan, John, 94, 160
Moore, Maurice A., 10, 94,
    162
Murphy, Patrick T., 41, 160

N

National Institute of Justice, 4,
    41, 91, 104, 143
National Institute of Juvenile
    Justice and Delinquency
    Prevention, 4, 13, 26, 57
Neighborhoods, changing
    characteristics of, 35-41

changing police contact rates
    by, 35-36
changing seriousness rates,
    35-36
classified as
    delinquency/crime
    producing, 44-47
consistency of careers in,
    47-54
continuity of careers in,
    47-54
distribution of
    delinquency/crime, by,
    30-35
milieu and
    delinquency/crime, 47-53
Nye, F. Ivan, 20, 162

O

Occupation, of parents, 22
Offender types, composition of,
    97-99, 148
    predicting adult from
    juvenile, 110-116
Offender typologies, 113-116
Offenders, ecological clustering
    by seriousness, 13-16
    increasing seriousness of,
    30-31, 35-38
    measures of seriousness of,
    13-14
    Part I and offender types,
    99-104
    type seriousness scores of,
    13-14
    typology construction using,
    93-97. 100-104, 105-116,
    148
Offense, rates and target
    density, 30-31

171

Printed in the United States
by Baker & Taylor Publisher Services